17375

P9-DFM-748

WITHDRAWN

Taylor 1/15/74

THE SONG LIST

THE SONG LIST

A Guide to Contemporary Music
From Classical Sources

Edited by
JAMES L. LIMBACHER
Audiovisual Librarian
Henry Ford Centennial Library
Dearborn, Michigan

THE PIERIAN PRESS
Ann Arbor, Michigan
1973

Library of Congress Catalog Card No. 73-78293
ISBN 0-87650-041-6

©Copyright 1973, James L. Limbacher
All Rights Reserved

The Pierian Press
P.O. Box 1808
Ann Arbor, MI. 48106

PREFACE

THE SONG LIST was compiled as a reference work to aid in (1) tracing the source of popular songs derived from classical themes, (2) discovering what classical themes are used in ballets, (3) identifying the theme songs of dance bands, radio programs and television series, and (4) helping to answer questions concerning these sources.

Now these answers have been indexed together into handy book form for the first time. We hope you will find it valuable. As always, we appreciate additions, corrections and suggestions from those who use it.

James L. Limbacher

KEY

Contemporary titles of works (songs, ballets, program themes, etc.) are listed by name in alphabetical order in the first column, followed in the next column by adapter, arranger or lyricist. The third column lists the original composer, and the last column gives the source work by that composer.

A second index groups the material by original composer and source, followed by the contemporary title.

Title	Adapter/Lyricist
"THE A & P GYPSIES" THEME	unlisted
A MOI LES PLASIRS	J. Barbier
	M. Carre
	H. Charley
"ABIE'S IRISH ROSE" THEME	unlisted
ACCEPT OUT THANKS	W. Hudson
ACCORDING TO THE BAEDEKER	C. Warnick
	M. Pahl
	I. Kostal
	E. Eager
ADELAIDE ON LA LANGAGE DES FLEURS	ballet
ADIEU VALSE	unlisted
ADMIRAL'S BOOGIE	C. Warnick
	M. Pahl
ADRIFT ON A STAR	E. Harburg
"ADVENTURES OF MCGRAW" THEME	J. Mercer
AEOLIAN HARP	unlisted
AFTER TODAY	W. Hanighen
	J. Blackton
AFTERNOON DREAM	J. Lawrence
	F. Spielman
AGITATION	unlisted
AH, DEATH THE STILL COOL NIGHT WILL BE	M. Spicker
	H. Heine

Composer	Source
A. Salama	Two Guitars
C. Gounod	unlisted
C. Olcott	My Wild Irish Rose
J. Sibelius	Finlandia
J. Strauss	A Night in Venice
M. Ravel	Valses Noble et Sentimentales
F. Chopin	Waltz 9 in A flat (Op. 69)
A. Sullivan	HMS Pinafore
J. Offenbach	Tales of Hoffman (Barcarolle)
H. Arlen	One for My Baby
F. Chopin	Etude 1 in A flat (Op. 25)
O. Straus	The Chocolate Soldier
C. Debussy	Afternoon of a Faun
F. Mendelssohn	Piano Piece in g (Op. 53, #3)
J. Brahms	unlisted

Title	Adapter/Lyricist
AH WELL A DAY	C. Warnick
	M. Pahl
AIR FOR THE G STRING	unlisted
AL 'N YETTA	A. Sherman
THE ALDER TREE BEFORE MY WINDOW	G. Galina
	G. Farrar
"THE ALDRICH FAMILY" THEME	D. Fields
ALL HAIL THE EMPRESS	R. Wright
	G. Forrest
ALL MY LIFE	unlisted
ALL MY LOVE	M. Parish
ALL MY LOVE	H. Askt
	S. Chaplin
	A. Jolson
ALL PEOPLE THAT ON EARTH DO DWELL	W. Kethe
	E. Barnes
ALL THAT GLITTERS	C. Warnick
	M. Pahl
ALL THE LIVELONG DAY	W. Herman
	T. Tyler
	A. Stillman
ALLEGRO BRILLIANTE	ballet
ALLELUJAH	unlisted
ALMIGHTY LORD	F. Manley
ALWAYS YOU	S. Robin
	W. Jason
"AMOS 'N' ANDY THEME	unlisted

4

Composer	Source
A. Sullivan	HMS Pinafore
J. S. Bach	Suite in D
traditional (France)	Allouette
S. Rachmaninoff	unlisted
A. Schwartz	This Is It
S. Rachmaninoff	Symphony 1
E. Waldteufel	Dolores Waltz
P. Durand	Boléro
E. Waldteufel	unlisted
J. S. Bach	Cantata 28
A. Sullivan	HMS Pinafore
G. Verdi	unlisted
P. Tchaikovsky	Piano Concerto 3
J. Haydn	Symphony 30 in C
P. Mascagni	Cavalleria Rusticanna (Intermezzo)
P. Tchaikovsky	Symphony 6 in b
C. Lucas	The Perfect Song

Title	Adapter/Lyricist
AND STILL THE VOLGA FLOWS	M. Willson
AND THAT REMINDS ME	unlisted
AND THE ANGELS SING	J. Mercer
	Z. Elman
AND THIS IS MY BELOVED	G. Forrest
ANGEL'S SERENADE	A. Wette
ANITRA'S BOOGIE	J. Grier
	M. Wright
	J. Wolf
ANITRA SWINGS	J. Wolf
	H. Moss
	L. Garisto
ANNIVERSARY SONG	S. Chaplin
	A. Jolson
ANNIVERSARY WALTZ see ANNIVERSARY SONG	
ANOTHER MAY SONG	T. Baker
	A. Dorffel
ANTAR	unlisted
ANTHEM FOR SPRING	S. Spaeth
ANTIQUES	C. Warnick
	C. Leigh
ANVIL PARADE	J. Tarto
ANYA	R. Wright
	G. Forrest
ANYMORE	unlisted
ANYONE CAN SEE	G. Lessner
	R. Sour

Composer	Source
S. Rachmaninoff	Piano Concerto 2
C. Bargoni	Autumn Concerto
traditional	Hebrew folk tune
A. Borodin	Prince Igor (duet)
E. Humperdinck	Hansel and Gretel
E. Grieg	Peer Gynt
E. Grieg	Peer Gynt
J. Ivanovici	Danube Waves (Donauwellen)
F. Mendelssohn	Witches' Song
N. Rimsky-Korsakov	Symphony 2
P. Mascagni	Cavelleria Rusticanna (Intermezzo)
R. Schumann	unlisted
G. Verdi	Il Trovatore
S. Rachmaninoff	Piano Concerto 1; Etudes Tableaux 2 (Op. 33)
traditional	Little Ball of Yarn
J. Strauss	unlisted

Title	Adapter/Lyricist
APART	G. Vail
APPASSIONATA	unlisted
APRIL IN THE RAIN	J. Klenner
APRIL NOSTALGIA	A. Ronell
APRIL SNOWBELL	M. Gould
"ARABESQUE" THEME	unlisted
ARABESQUE COOKIE	D. Ellington B. Strayhorn
ARABIAN NIGHTMARE	L. Singer
ARABIAN NIGHTS	A. Alexander
ARCHDUKE TRIO	unlisted
ARIADNE'S LAMENT	unlisted
"ARTHUR GODFREY TIME" THEME	J. J. Loeb
AS YEARS GO BY	C. Tobias
ASIA MAJOR	J. Wisner
ASIA MINOR	unlisted
AT CHRISTMASTIME	G. Forrest R. Wright
AT MAXIM'S	M. Pahl C. Warnick V. Leon L. Stein C. Leigh

Composer	Source
F. Chopin	Prelude in A, No. 7 (Op. 28)
L. Beethoven	Sonata for Piano 23 in f (Op. 57)
F. Chopin	Nocturne 1 (Op. 9)
O. Strauss	unlisted
P. Tchaikovsky	The Months
N. Rimsky-Korsakov	Scheherazade
P. Tchaikovsky	Nutcracker Suite (Arabian Dance)
N. Rimsky-Korsakov	Scheherazade
N. Rimsky-Korsakov	Scheherazade
L. Beethoven	Trio for Piano and Strings 7 in B Flat
P. Locatelli	Concerto Grosso (Op. 7, #6)
C. Lombardo	Seems Like Old Times
J. Brahms	Hungarian Dance 4
F. Chopin	unlisted
E. Grieg	Piano Concerto in a
E. Grieg	Woodland Wanderings
F. Lehar	The Merry Widow

9

Title	Adapter/Lyricist
AT NIGHT	L. Clough
	E. Engel
AT NIGHT ON THE RIVER	A. Mirovitch
AT THE CROSSROADS	R. Russell
AT THE FOLIES BERGERE	M. Pahl
	C. Warnick
	I. Kostal
AT THE GATES OF KANBALU	M. Pahl
	C. Warnick
	I. Kostal
AT THE ZOO	A. Gamse
AT TIMES MY THOUGHTS GO DRIFTING	V. Harris
	K. Croth
	R. Chapman
	C. Robinson
AU REVOIR, SOLDIER	J. Latouche
AUGUST HARVEST SONG	M. Gould
"AUNT JENNY" THEME	unlisted
AURORA'S WEDDING	ballet
AUTOMATION	A. Sherman
AUTUMN REVERIE	unlisted
AUTUMN SONG	unlisted
AVALON	B. deSylva
	V. Rose
	A. Jolson
BABEL	N. Shilkret
BABY GOTTA HAVE A LITTLE FUN	H. Blake
	J. Yellen
"THE BABY SNOOKS SHOW" THEME	unlisted

Composer	Source
S. Rachmaninoff	Six Songs
D. Kabalevsky	unlisted
E. Lecuona	Malagueña
J. Strauss	unlisted
N. Rimsky- Korsakov	unlisted
E. Grieg	Norwegian Dances
J. Brahms	unlisted
F. Chopin	Mazurka in Bb
P. Tchaikovsky	The Months
traditional	Believe Me, If All Those Endearing Young Charms
P. Tchaikovsky	Sleeping Beauty (Act III)
F. Marchetti	Waltz Tzigane
C. Chaminade	Autumn
F. Chopin	The Maiden's Wish (Zyczenie)
G. Puccini	Tosca (E lucevan le stelle)
I. Stravinsky	unlisted
H. Alfven	Swedish Polka
traditional	Rock-a-Bye Baby

Title	Adapter/Lyricist
BACH GOES TO PARIS	F. Loffler
BACH GOES TO TOWN	N. Hefti
BACH GOES TO TOWN	A. Templeton
BACH MAMBO	E. Bradford
BACH MEETS THE BULLS	F. Loffler
BACH REVISITED	E. Safranski
BACH TO THE BLUES	R. Lewis
BACH VISITS THE CAFE ROUGE	R. Maltby
BACH'S BAG	F. Loffler
BACH'S BEDROOM BREW	F. Loffler
BACH'S MASHED BOURREE	F. Loffler
"BACHELOR'S CHILDREN" THEME	R. J. Young
BACHOMANIA	F. Loffler
BACKBEAT SYMPHONY	unlisted
"BACKSTAGE WIFE" THEME	C. Spencer
THE BAGPIPES	unlisted
BALALAIKA SERENADE	F. Steininger F. Brown
THE BALLAD OF HARRY LEWIS	A. Sherman
BALLERINA	L. Bryant J. Klenner
BALLERINA	F. LaForge G. Toupin
BALLET CHA CHA CHA	H. Harden
BALLET IMPERIAL	ballet

Composer	Source
J. S. Bach	French Suite 5 (Gavotte)
J. S. Bach	unlisted
J. S. Bach	unlisted
J. S. Bach	Fugue for Organ
J. S. Bach	English Suite 5 (Saraband)
J. S. Bach	unlisted
J. S. Bach	Sleepers Awake
J. S. Bach	unlisted
J. S. Bach	Partita 4 (Aria)
J. S. Bach	Suite for Orchestra 3 (Overture)
J. S. Bach	Violin Partita 1
V. Herbert	Ah, Sweet Mystery of Life
J. S. Bach	Invention 13
P. Tchaikovsky	Symphony 5
C. Glover	Rose of Tralee
J. Haydn	Dance 16
P. Tchaikovsky	June Barcarolle/Serenade (The Months)
W. Steffe	Battle Hymn of the Republic
F. Chopin	Waltz 6 (Op. 64) (Minute Waltz)
L. Delibes	unlisted
A. Ponchielli	La Gioconda
P. Tchaikovsky	Piano Concerto 2

13

Title	Adapter/Lyricist
BANJO	J. Morross
BARBERING BIZET	L. Addeo
BARCA ROCK 'N ROLL	A. Datz J. Barbier
BARCAROLLE	unlisted
BARCAROLLE BLARNEY	F. Black J. Barbier
BARKY ROLL STOMP	J. Busek J. Barbier
BAUBLES, BANGLES AND BEADS	R. Wright G. Forrest
BE GLAD THERE'S A HOLE IN YOUR HEAD	P. Weston O. Nash
BE MINE	H. Fields D. O'Connor
BE SHE DARK, BE SHE FAIR	E. Maschwitz B. Grun
BE STILL MY SOUL	K. VonSchlegel
THE BEAR SYMPHONY	unlisted
THE BEAR WENT OVER THE MOUNTAIN	traditional
BEAT OUT DAT RHYTHM ON A DRUM	O. Hammerstein II
BEAUTIFUL NIGHT	unlisted
THE BEE'S WEDDING	unlisted
BEETHOVEN BOUNCE	A. Donahue
BEETHOVEN'S FIFTH	J. Melis

Composer	Source
L. Gottschalk	The Banjo
G. Bizet	Carmen
J. Offenbach	Tales of Hoffman (Barcarolle)
D. Scarlatti	Sonata for Piano (L. 132)
J. Offenbach	Tales of Hoffman (Barcarolle)
J. Offenbach	Tales of Hoffman (Barcarolle)
A. Borodin	String Quartet 2
S. Prokofiew	Peter and the Wolf
S. Yradier	La Paloma
A. Dvorak	unlisted
J. Sibelius	Finlandia
J. Haydn	Symphony 82 in C
L. Beethoven	Wellington's Victory
G. Bizet	Carmen (Carmen Jones)
J. Offenbach	Tales of Hoffman (Barcarolle)
F. Mendelssohn	Song Without Words (Op. 67)
L. Beethoven	Symphony 5
L. Beethoven	Symphony 5

Title	Adapter/Lyricist
BEFORE	S. Camarata
	R. Connelly
THE BELLS	R. Kountz
	G. Purcell
BELLS OF MOSCOW	unlisted
BELOVED LAND	M. Andrews
BENDELSSOHN'S SPRING SONG	A. Templeton
BESIDE A LITTLE BROOK	G. Vail
	E. Lester
"BETTY AND BOB" THEME	unlisted
"BETWEEN THE BOOKENDS" THEME	unlisted
"BIG JOHN AND SPARKY" THEME	S. Cahn
	S. Chaplin
"BIG SISTER" THEME	unlisted
THE BIRD	unlisted
BIZET HAS HIS DAY	L. Brown
BIZZY BIZET	N. Perito
	H. Meilhac
BLACK AND BLUE DANUBE	S. Jones
BLACK KEY	unlisted
BLACK VELVET SKY	M. Kahn
	J. Fina
	O. Shelley
BLACKSMITH RAG	H. Pinder
	W. Garton
	L. Wood
BLITHE BELLS	P. Grainger

Composer	Source
S. Rachmaninoff	Piano Concerto 2
S. Rachmaninoff	Prelude in c sharp
S. Rachmaninoff	Prelude in c sharp
J. Sibelius	Finlandia
F. Mendelssohn	Piano Piece in A (Op. 62, #6)
J. Brahms	May Valse
E. Elgar	Salut d'Amour
traditional	Auld Lange Syne
J. Bratton	The Teddy Bear's Parade
R. Drigo	Valse Bluette
J. Haydn	String Quartet in C (Op. 33, #3)
G. Bizet	L'Arlesienne Suite
G. Bizet	Carmen
J. Strauss	Blue Danube Waltz
F. Chopin	Etude 5 in G flat (Op. 10)
F. Chopin	unlisted
G. Verdi	Il Trovatore (Anvil Chorus)
J. S. Bach	unlisted

Title	Adapter/Lyricist
BLUE DANUBE CHA CHA	M. D'Agay
BLUE DANUBE DREAM	H. Salter
	G. Kahn
BLUE DANUBE GOES DIXIELAND	P. Napoleon
BLUE DANUBE LAMENT	S. Kuller
BLUE DANUBE SWING	S. Philips
BLUE DANUBE ROCK	B. Harding
BLUE REEDS	M. Rogers
BLUE IS MY HEART	B. Davis
	A. Silver
BLUE RIVER ROCK	M. Manning
	D. Davis
"THE BOB BURNS SHOW" THEME	unlisted
"THE BOB HOPE SHOW" THEME	L. Robin
THE BOGEY BAYOU REVIVAL	R. Benninghoff
BOLERO	A. Dubensky
	A. DeMusset
BON VIVANT	R. Wright
	G. Forrest
BORODIN'S BOUNCE	L. Brown
	J. Hill
THE BOSSA INDIA	L. Brown
	J. Hill
BRAHMS FOR THE CRADLE SET	S. Henderson
BRAHMS IN BLUES	A. Datz
THE BREEZE AND I	A. Stillman
BRIGHT SKIES ARE EVERYWHERE	C. Willard
	A. Payne

Composer	Source
J. Strauss	Blue Danube Waltz
J. Strauss	Blue Danube Waltz
J. Strauss	Blue Danube Waltz
J. Strauss	Blue Danube Waltz
J. Strauss	Blue Danube Waltz
J. Strauss	Blue Danube Waltz
P. Tchaikovsky	Nutcracker Suite (Dance of the Reed Flutes)
C. Saint-Saens	The Swan (La Cygne)
F. Mendelssohn	unlisted
traditional	The Arkansas Traveler
R. Rainger	Thanks for the Memory
L. Beethoven	Symphony 6
F. Delius	Les Filles de Cadiz
E. Grieg	To a Water Lily
A. Borodin	String Quartet 2 in D
N. Rimsky-Korsakov	Song of India
J. Brahms	Cradle Song
J. Brahms	unlisted
E. Lecuona	Andalucia
F. Schubert	unlisted

Title	Adapter/Lyricist
BROKEN MELODY	S. Spaeth
BRUNSWICK MAINE	E. Eager
	H. Meilhac
THE BULLFINCH	unlisted
THE BUMBLE BEAT	D. Roman
	A. Pellegrini
	T. Waldman
BUMBLING BUMBLEBEE	S. Miller
	R. Gilbert
	W. Scharf
THE BUSY BEE	E. Eager
	H. Meilhac
BUTTERFLY	unlisted
BY THE SLEEPY LAGOON see SLEEPY LAGOON	
THE CAGE	ballet
CAN-CAN BOOGIE	R. Block
	P. Swain
CAN-CAN POLKA	J. Biviano
CANARY CAPRICE	D. Liebert
CANDLE SYMPHONY	unlisted
CARACOLE	ballet
DE CARDS DON'T LIE	R. Bennett
	O. Hammerstein II
	H. Meilhac
	L. Halevy
CARMEN	ballet
CARMEN BOOGIE	various

Composer	Source
J. Sibelius	unlisted
J. Offenbach	Orpheus in the Underworld
D. Scarlatti	Sonata for Piano (L. 488)
N. Rimsky-Korsakov	Flight of the Bumble Bee
N. Rimsky-Korsakov	Flight of the Bumble Bee
J. Offenbach	Orpheus in the Underworld
F. Chopin	Etude in G flat (Op.25)
I. Stravinsky	Concerto Grosso in D
J. Offenbach	Gaîté Parisienne
J. Offenbach	Gaîté Parisienne
N. Paganini	Perpetual Motion
J. Haydn	Symphony 45 in f Sharp
W. Mozart	Divertmento 15
G. Bizet	Carmen (Carmen Jones)
G. Bizet	Carmen
G. Bizet	Carmen

Title	Adapter/Lyricist
CARMEN CAPERS	F. Black
	H. Meilhac
	L. Halevy
CARMEN ON A SPREE	R. Linda
	H. Meilhac
	L. Halevy
CARMEN'S CHA CHA	C. Mostroni
CARMEN'S TANGO	R. Flanagan
CARNIVAL FOR LIFE	R. Bodanzky
	A. Ross
	B. Hood
	A. Wilner
CARTWHEEL	unlisted
CASHIER'S LAMENT	S. Meyer
	E. Brandt
	H. Meilhac
	L. Halevy
CASTLE OF DREAMS	J. McCarthy
CASTLES IN THE AIR see CASTLE OF DREAMS	
CAT DUET	C. Colette
CAT'S FUGUE	A. Kramer
CAVALRY OF THE STEPPES	B. Homer
CHACUN A SON GOUT	H. Dietz
CHALLENGE	G. Farrar
CHARLEY'S DREAM	C. Dant
CHARMIN CARMEN	B. Home
	H. Meilhac
	L. Halevy

Composer	Source
G. Bizet	Carmen
G. Bizet	Carmen
G. Bizet	Carmen
G. Bizet	Carmen
F. Lehar	The Count of Luxembourg
F. Chopin	Etude 3 in F (Op. 25)
G. Bizet	Carmen
F. Chopin	Waltz 6 in D flat
M. Ravel	L'Enfant et les Sortelieges
D. Scarlatti	Sonata in g
traditional (Russian)	Soviet Army Song
J. Strauss	Fledermaus
P. Tchaikovsky	Symphony 6 in b
N. Rimsky-Korsakov	Scheherazade
G. Bizet	Carmen

Title	Adapter/Lyricist
CHEEK TO CHEEK	I. Berlin
CHEERS FOR THE HERO	E. Harburg
	J. Gorney
	R. de Cormier
"CHESTERFIELD SUPPER CLUB" THEME	unlisted
CHINA WHERE	M. Rogers
CHINOISERIE	D. Ellington
	B. Strayhorn
CHO CHO SAN	unlisted
CHOPIN IN THE CITRUS BELT	E. Harris
CHOPPIN' AT CHOPIN	L. Garisto
	J. Wolf
	J. Moss
CHOPPIN' CHOPIN	unlisted
CHOPSTICKS	unlisted
CHRIST THE LORD IS RISEN TODAY	J.Gilette
	C. Wesley
CHRISTMAS LIST	P. Lee
THE CHRISTMAS TREE	E. Biggs
THE CHURCH'S ONE FOUNDATION	S. Stone
CLING TO ME	M. David
	J. Livingston
	A. Hoffman

24

Composer	Source
F. Chopin	Polonaise 6 in A flat
J. Offenbach	unlisted
R. Ringwald	A Cigarette, Sweet Music and You
P. Tchaikovsky	Nutcracker Suite (Chinese Dance)
P. Tchaikovsky	Nutcracker Suite (Chinese Dance)
G. Puccini	Madama Butterfly (Un Bel Di)
F. Chopin	unlisted
F. Chopin	Waltz 7 in c Sharp
F. Chopin	Fantasie Impromptu in c Sharp
A. Borodin	Paraphrases for Four Hands
C. Cui	
A. Liadoff	
N. Rimsky-Korsakov	
W. A. Mozart	traditional hymn
J. Haydn	Symphony 93 (2nd movement)
F. Liszt	Piano Suite (2nd movement)
M. Haydn	unlisted
J. Brahms	unlisted

Title	Adapter/Lyricist
THE CLOCK SYMPHONY	unlisted
THE COCKCROW	unlisted
COFFEE CANTATA	unlisted
COLORATURA WALTZ	G. Lessner
	R. Sour
COLUMBIA, THE GEM OF THE OCEAN	unlisted
COME SOON	J. Harrison
COME TO ME	A. Askanoff
COME TO THE DANCE	G. Clutson
	M. Mervyn
COMES THE REVOLUTION	E. Eager
	H. Meilhac
CON AMORE	ballet
CONCERTO BAROCCO	ballet
CONCERTO FOR TWO	J. Lawrence
CONFIDENCE	unlisted
CONSOLATION	unlisted
CONTEMPLATION	unlisted
CORELLI IN THE OLD CORRAL	A. Templeton
CORTEGE	unlisted

Composer	Source
J. Haydn	Symphony 101 in D
L. Beethoven	Sonata for Violin 10 in G (Op. 96)
J. S. Bach	Cantata 211
J. Strauss	unlisted
T. à Becket	Britannia, The Pride of the Ocean
J. Brahms	unlisted
L. Beethoven	unlisted
C. Weber	Invitation to the Dance
J. Offenbach	Orpheus in the Underworld
G. Rossini	Overtures from La Gazza Ladra, El Signor Bruschino, La Scala di Seta
J. S. Bach	Concerto for Two Violins
P. Tchaikovsky	Piano Concerto 1 in b flat
F. Mendelssohn	Piano Piece in A (Op. 19 #4)
F. Mendelssohn	Piano Piece in E (Op. 30 #3)
F. Mendelssohn	Piano Piece in E flat (Op. 30, #1)
A. Corelli	unlisted
D. Scarlatti	Sonata for Piano (L. 23)

Title	Adapter/Lyricist
COTTON PICKIN' CARMEN	V. Alexander
	H. Meilhac
	L. Halevy
COTTON TAIL	E. Maschwitz
	B. Grun
"COUNTRY MUSIC JUBILEE" THEME	unlisted
CREATION	J. Addison
CROSSROADS	
see AT THE CROSSROADS	
THE CUCKOO AND THE NIGHTINGALE	unlisted
CUCKOO CONCERTO	unlisted
CUTE AND SASSY	B. Leighton
	M. Wechsler
DA-DA-DA-DAAH	R. Benninghoff
DANCE FOR YOUNG LOVERS	J. Harnell
DANCE OF THE FLOREADORES	D. Ellington
	B. Strayhorn
DANCE OF THE MATADOR	D. Walker
DANCE OF THE ORANGE TARTS	H. Hisselberg
DANCE OF THE SKELETONS	W. Liberace
DANCE FOR WALT WHITMAN	ballet
DANCE FOR YOUNG LOVERS	J. Harnell
DANCING DOLL	G. Liberace
DANCING SKELETONS	G. Robinson
DANNY BOY	unlisted
"THE DANNY THOMAS SHOW" THEME	unlisted

Composer	Source
G. Bizet	Carmen
A. Dvorak	Symphony 9 (New World)
H. Garland	Sugarfoot Rag
F. Haydn	The Creation
G. Handel	Concerto for Organ 13 in F
A. Vivaldi	Concerto for Violin
G. Verdi	Rigoletto (Caro Nome)
L. Beethoven	Symphony 5
P. Tchaikovsky	unlisted
P. Tchaikovsky	Nutcracker Suite (Waltz of the Flowers)
M. deFalla	El Amor Brujo (Ritual Fire Dance)
P. Tchaikovsky	Nutcracker Suite
C. Saint-Saens	Danse Macabre
D. Diamond	Rounds for Orchestra
P. Tchaikovsky	Nutcracker Suite
A. Ponchielli	La Gioconda
C. Saint-Saens	Danse Macabre
traditional	Londonderry Air
traditional	Londonderry Air

Title	Adapter/Lyricist
DANS TON COEUR	M. Pahl
	C. Warnick
	I. Kostal
	E. Eager
DANSE BOHEMIENNE	various
DANSE EXPRESSO COFFEE	M. Rogers
DANSE MISTIQUE	R. Lewis
DANSE ORIENTALE	F. Kreisler
DANUBE BY MOONLIGHT	M. Pahl
	C. Warnick
	I. Kostal
DARK ELEGIES	ballet
DAT'S LOVE	O. Hammerstein II
	H. Meilhac
	L. Halevy
	R. Bennett
"DAVID HARUM" THEME	W. Cobb
DAYBREAK	H. Adamson
DAYDREAMING OF A NIGHT	M. Witty
	E. McNaughton
DEAD RAT BLUES	M. Pahl
	C. Warnick
	I. Kostal
DEAR LAND OF HOME	C. Manney
DEAR ONE	J. Harnell
DEATH AND THE MAIDEN	unlisted
DEBUSSY'S DREAM	L. Brown
	J. Hill

Composer	Source
J. Strauss	unlisted
G. Bizet	The Fair Maid of Perth
P. Tchaikovsky	unlisted
P. Tchaikovsky	Nutcracker Suite (Arabian Dance)
N. Rimsky-Korsakov	Scheherazade
J. Strauss	unlisted
G. Mahler	Kindertotenlieder
G. Bizet	Carmen (Carmen Jones)
G. Edwards	Sunbonnet Sue
F. Grofe	Mississippi Suite
P. Tchaikovsky	Swan Lake (Act II)
J. Strauss	unlisted
J. Sibelius	Finlandia
P. Tchaikovsky	Romeo and Juliet
F. Schubert	Quartet for Strings 14 (Op. 161)
C. Debussy	Reverie

Title	Adapter/Lyricist
DEDICATION	T. Mossman
DEEP BLUE EVENING	E. Maschwitz
	B. Grun
DEPARTURE	L. Untermeyer
DERE'S A CAFE ON DE CORNER	O. Hammerstein II
	R. Bennett
	H. Meilhac
	L. Halevy
DESIGNS WITH STRING	ballet
DEVIL DANCE	H. Sukman
THE DEVIL'S TRILL	unlisted
DIM LUSTRE	ballet
DINGBAT, THE SINGING CAT	T. Mossman
DINNA MARIE	A. Wreubel
DO WE HAVE TO SAY GOODNIGHT?	M. David
	J. Livingston
	A. Hoffman
DO YOU LIKE BRAHMS?	
	D. Sonneborn
"DR. CHRISTIAN" THEME	P. F. Webster
DOG WALTZ	unlisted
"DON WINSLOW OF THE NAVY" THEME	unlisted
DONKEY SERENADE	R. Wright
	G. Forrest
DON'T EVER LET ME GO	T. Mossman
	M. Parish
DON'T EVER TAKE A HOLIDAY	B. Adlam

Composer	Source
R. Schumann	Widmung
A. Dvorak	Symphony 9 (New World)
S. Prokofiev	Winter Holiday
G. Bizet	Carmen (Carmen Jones)
P. Tchaikovsky	Trio in a (2nd movement)
F. Liszt	Mephisto Waltz
G. Tartini	Sonata for Violin in g
R. Strauss	Burleske for Piano and Orchestra
S. Prokofiew	Peter and the Wolf
C. Debussy	Nuit d'Etoilles
J. Brahms	unlisted
J. Brahms	unlisted
L. Alter	Rainbow on the River
F. Chopin	Waltz 1 in D flat (Op. 64)
T. à Becket	Britannia, the Pride of the Ocean
R. Friml	Sympathy
P. Tchaikovsky	unlisted
J. Offenbach	unlisted

Title	Adapter/Lyricist
DON'T YOU KNOW	B. Worth
DORIAN	unlisted
DORIE	unlisted
DREAM, DREAM, DREAM	A. Hoffman
DREAM ENTHRALLING	H. Clutsam
	A. Ross
DREAM OF LOVE	various
DREAM OF LOVE	S. Romberg
DREAM QUARTET	unlisted
DREAMING	M. Zeiteberger
DREAMS	D. Costa
	A. Ferrante
	L. Teicher
DREAMS OF LOVE AND YOU	unlisted
DRIVE WITH CARE	W. Wirges
	H. Meilhac
DROWSY BABY	L. Roberts
	M. Gabriel
	J. Callahan
DRUM ROLL SYMPHONY	unlisted
"DUFFY'S TAVERN" THEME	unlisted
DUMKY TRIO	unlisted
DVORAK'S LETTER HOME	E. Maschwitz
	B. Grun
EASTERN ROMANCE	O. Langey
"THE EASY ACES" THEME	unlisted

Composer	Source
G. Puccini	La Bohéme (Musetta's Waltz Song)
J. S. Bach	Toccata and Fugue in d
traditional	Dodi Li
F. Liszt	unlisted
F. Schubert	unlisted
F. Liszt	Liebestraum
F. Schubert	Liebestraum
J. Haydn	String Quartet in F (Op. 50, #5)
R. Schumann	Traumerei
R. Schumann	Traumerei
F. Liszt	Liebestraum
G. Bizet	Carmen
G. Movel	Norwegian Cradle Song
J. Haydn	Symphony 103 in E flat
E. Ball	When Irish Eyes Are Smiling
A. Dvorak	Trio in e (Op. 90)
A. Dvorak	unlisted
N. Rimsky-Korsakov	unlisted
L. Alter	Manhattan Serenade

Title	Adapter/Lyricist
EBONY RHAPSODY	L. Franz
	S. Coslow
	A. Johnson
ECHO	unlisted
THE ECHO TOLD ME A LIE	H. Barnes
	H. Fields
	D. John
	P. Jack
"THE ED SULLIVAN SHOW" THEME	unlisted
"THE EDDIE CANTOR SHOW" THEME	unlisted
"THE EDDIE FISHER SHOW" THEME	unlisted
THE EGYPTIAN CONCERTO	unlisted
THE EIFFEL TOWER	M. Pahl
	C. Warnick
	I. Kostal
THE ELEPHANT	O. Nash
ELISE	J. Noble
	L. Singer
EMANUEL	W. Robertson
	C. Miles
EMPEROR CONCERTO	unlisted
THE EMPEROR WALTZ	J. Burke
EMPTY CHAIR	ballet
ENCORE MELODY	A. Stillman
	A. Green
END OF THE LOVE AFFAIR	C. Warnick
	M. Pahl

Composer	Source
F. Liszt	Rhapsody 2
A. Vivaldi	Concerto for String Orchestra in A
P. Tchaikovsky	unlisted
R. Bloch	Toast of the Town
R. Whiting	One Hour With You
J. Styne	As Long As There's Music
C. Saint-Saens	Piano Concerto 5 in F (Op. 103)
J. Strauss	unlisted
C. Saint-Saens	Carnival of the Animals
L. Beethoven	Für Elise
F. Chopin	unlisted
L. Beethoven	Piano Concerto 5 in E flat (Op. 73)
J. Strauss	Emperor Waltz
N. Keyes	Suite
P. Mascagni	Cavalleria Rusticanna (Intermezzo)
J. Strauss	unlisted

Title	Adapter/Lyricist
ENIGMA VARIATIONS	unlisted
EPISODES	ballet
THE ERL-KING	various
EROICA SYMPHONY	unlisted
EROS	O. Benzon
	H. Schmidt
	N. Dole
THE ERROR-ATTICA	R. Benninghoff
"ESCAPE" THEME	unlisted
ESCAPE IT ALL	E. Eager
	C. Warnick
	M. Pahl
	I. Kostal
ETERNAL GOD, OUR FATHER	B. Miller
	O. Davis
ETERNALLY	G. Parsons
"ETHEL AND ALBERT" THEME	unlisted
EUREKA	E. Harburg
EVENING BELLS	S. Salter
EVENING CONCERTO	J. Wisner
EVENING FAIR	P. Bourget
	F. Martens
EVENING HYMN	T. Ken
EVENING SONG	F. Joslyn
EVENING STAR	unlisted

Composer	Source
E. Elgar	Variations for Orchestra (Op. 36)
A. Webern	Ricercata and Opus 1, 10 and 24
F. Schubert	Der Erlkonig
L. Beethoven	Symphony 3
E. Grieg	Erotik
L. Beethoven	Symphony 3
M. Mussorgsky	A Night on Bald Mountain
J. Strauss	The Gypsy Baron
J. Sibelius	Finlandia
C. Chaplin	Limelight (film theme)
L. Hirsch O. Harbach	Love Nest
J. Offenbach	Bluebeard
C. Saint-Saens	unlisted
P. Tchaikovsky	Piano Concerto 1 in b flat
C. Debussy	Beau Soir
T. Tallis	Tallis' Canon
L. Beethoven	Piano Sonata 14
F. Mendelssohn	Piano Piece in E flat (Op. 38, #1)

Title	Adapter/Lyricist
EVERYTIME I TRY TO SAY GOODBYE	J. Barbier M. Pahl C. Warnick
"THE FBI IN PEACE AND WAR" THEME	unlisted
FAITH	unlisted
"THE FAMILY HOUR"	unlisted
FANFARE	ballet
FANTASY	T. Mossman
FAR INTO THE NIGHT	B. Knoll I. Fields M. Rich
FAR INTO THE NIGHT	M. David J. Livingston A. Hoffman
FAREWELL SYMPHONY	unlisted
FAREWELL TO SPRING see SHALL WE SAY FAREWELL	
FASCINATION	R. Manning
FATE	R. Wright G. Forrest
FATE SYMPHONY	unlisted
FEATS OF THE PIPER	I. Taylor H. Stanley
FIGARO FLIP	G. Kingsley
FIGURE IN THE CARPET	ballet
FIRE SYMPHONY	unlisted

40

Composer	Source
J. Offenbach	Tales of Hoffman
S. Prokofiev	Love for Three Oranges (March)
F. Mendelssohn	Piano Piece in C (Op. 102, #6)
C. Debussy	Clair de Lune
B. Britten	Young Person's Guide to the Orchestra
R. Schumann	Traumerei
G. Bizet	unlisted
J. Brahms	unlisted
J. Haydn	Symphony 45 in f Sharp
F. Marchetti	Waltz Tzigane
A. Borodin	Symphony 2 in b
L. Beethoven	Symphony 5
E. Grieg	Peer Gynt (Hall of the Mountain)
W. Mozart	Marriage of Figaro (Non piu andrai)
G. Handel	Royal Fireworks Music and Water Music
J. Haydn	Symphony 59

41

Title	Adapter/Lyricist
"THE FIRST NIGHTER" THEME	unlisted
"THE FIRST PIANO QUARTET" THEME	unlisted
THE "FIST" SYMPHONY	unlisted
FIVE MINUTES OF SPRING	E. Harburg R. deCormier J. Gorney J. Halevy H. Meilhac
FLASHY FINGERS	G. Galian
FLIM FLAM FLOO	I. Taylor H. Stanley
FLOW, RIVER, FLOW	J. Klenner
THE FLOWER	H. Clutsam
FLOWER WALTZ	F. Steininger F. Brown
FLOWERSVILLE	B. Kessel
FOLIES BERGERE	M. Pahl C. Warnick I. Kostal
FOOD FOR THOUGHT	E. Brandt S. Meyer
FOOL'S GOLD	I. Taylor H. Stanley
FOR EVERY LONELY HEART	H. Stothart
FOR LOVERS ONLY	J. Wisner
FOR THE LOVE OF A PRINCESS	R. Lewis
FOR THE LOVE OF ME	unlisted

Composer	Source
unlisted	Neopolitan Nights
N. Paganini	Variations
J. Haydn	Symphony 39 in g
J. Offenbach	Orpheus in the Underworld
C. Saint-Saens	unlisted
E. Grieg	Norwegian Dances
F. Chopin	Etude 3 (Op. 10)
F. Schubert	Lilac Time
P. Tchaikovsky	Nutcracker Suite (Waltz of the Flowers)
G. Bizet	Carmen (Flower Song)
J. Strauss	Can-Can
G. Verdi	unlisted
E. Grieg	Peer Gynt
P. Tchaikovsky	None But the Lonely Heart
F. Schubert	unlisted
N. Rimsky-Korsakov	Scheherazade
F. Chopin	Polonaise 6 in A flat

Title	Adapter/Lyricist
FOR THE SAKE OF ART	G. Lessner
	R. Sour
FOR THEE SUOMI	L. Clough
	M. Chase
FOR YOU	F. Cunkle
FORBIDDEN ORCHID	R. Wright
	G. Forrest
"FORD SUNDAY EVENING HOUR" THEME	unlisted
FOREVER LOVED	D. Costa
	A. Ferrante
	L. Teicher
FOUR JOLLY BROTHERS	A. Rose
FOUR TEMPERMENTS	ballet
THE FOUR TEMPERMENTS	unlisted
"THE FRED ALLEN SHOW"	B. Hooker
"THE FRED WARING SHOW"	unlisted
FREDDY AND HIS FIDDLE	R. Wright
	G. Forrest
THE FRENCH ROCK & ROLL	C. Warnick
	M. Pahl
	E. Eager
	I. Kostal
FRENCH SERENADE	G. Broch
FRIENDLY UNDERSTANDING	C. Warnick
	M. Pahl
THE FROG QUARTET	unlisted
FROM MY LIFE	unlisted
FROM THE NEW WORLD	unlisted

Composer	Source
J. Strauss	unlisted
J. Sibelius	Finlandia
J. Brahms	unlisted
H. Villa-Lobos	The Theft of the Madonna (Magdalena)
E. Humperdinck	Hansel and Gretel (Prayer)
P. Tchaikovsky	Romeo and Juliet
F. Schubert	unlisted
P. Hindemith	Theme and Four Variations
C. Nielsen	Symphony 2 in b
R. Friml	Smile, Darn Ya, Smile
unlisted	Sleep
E. Grieg	Norwegian Dances
J. Strauss	unlisted
E. Grieg	unlisted
J. Strauss	unlisted
J. Haydn	String Quartet in D (Op. 50, #6)
B. Smetana	Quartet for Strings 1 in e
A. Dvorak	Symphony 9 in E

Title	Adapter/Lyricist
FROM THE NORTH	J. Runeberg
	T. Baker
"FRONT PAGE FARRELL" THEME	A. Stillman
	L. Stallings
FULL MOON AND EMPTY ARMS	T. Mossman
FUNERAL MARCH	unlisted
FUNERAL SYMPHONY	unlisted
G MINOR CHA CHA	G. Kingsley
GAITE PARISIENNE	ballet
GALA PERFORMANCE	ballet
GALLOPADE	R. Bourdon
THE GARDENING OF IMAGINING	E. Eager
	M. Pahl
	C. Warnick
	I. Kostal
THE GARDEN OF LOVE	M. Keith
GAVOTTE	J. Latouche
	B. Kaper
GENTLY, LORD, O GENTLY LEAD US	N. Dett
"THE GEORGE GOBEL SHOW" THEME	unlisted
GESTICULATE	R. Wright
	G. Forrest
THE GHOST TRIO	unlisted
LA GIOCCONDA'S LAST DANCE	G. Sonneborn
A GIRL IS A NECESSARY TROUBLE	M. Liebman

46

Composer	Source
J. Sibelius	unlisted
A. Schwartz	You and I Know
S. Rachmaninoff	Piano Concerto 2
F. Mendelssohn	Piano Piece in e (Op. 62, #3)
J. Haydn	Symphony 44 in e
W. Mozart	Symphony 40 in g
J. Offenbach	Offenbach themes
S. Prokofiev	Piano Concerto 3 and Classical Symphony
G. Rossini	William Tell (Overture)
N. Rimsky-Korsakov	unlisted
N. Rimsky-Korsakov	Scheherazade
F. Chopin	Variations on a French Air
Welsh air (Bahama Folk Song)	All Through the Night
J. S. Trotter	Gobelues
A. Borodin	Symphony 1
L. Beethoven	Trio for Piano and Strings #5 in D
A. Ponchielli	La Gioconda
J. Strauss	The Gypsy Baron

Title	Adapter/Lyricist
THE GIRL WITH THE LIGHT BLUE HAIR	L. Whitcup
THE GIRL WITH THE YELLOW HAIR	H. Dietz
GLOOMY SUNDAY	S. Lewis
THE GLORY THAT WAS GREECE	E. Harburg
GOD SAVE THE QUEEN (KING)	unlisted
GOIN' HOME	W. Fisher
GOIN' WITH CARMEN	L. Garisto
	J. Wolf
	H. Moss
GOING HOME see GOIN' HOME	
GOLDBERG VARIATIONS	unlisted
"THE GOLDBERGS" THEME	unlisted
THE GOLDEN SONG	A. Ross
	H. Clutsam
GOODBYE	I. Caesar
GOODBYE AGAIN see SAY NO MORE, IT'S GOODBYE	
GRANADA	various
THE GRAND AND GLORIOUS FOURTH	G. Lessner
	R. Sour
GRANT THOSE GLANCES	unlisted
THE GREEK MARINES	E. Harburg
"THE GREEN HORNET" THEME	unlisted
GREEN STAMPS	A. Sherman
	L. Busch

48

Composer	Source
G. Marie	La Cinquantaine
J. Strauss	Fledermaus
R. Seress	Szomoru Vasarnap
J. Offenbach	La Belle Hélène
J. C. Bach	Harp Concerto in D (Allegro Moderato)
A. Dvorak	Symphony 9 (New World)
G. Bizet	Carmen (Habañera)
J. S. Bach	Air and 30 Variations
E. Toselli	Serenade
F. Schubert	Lilac Time
E. Coates	White Horse Inn
I. Albeniz	Spanish Suite
J. Strauss	unlisted
S. deFuentes	Miriame Asi
J. Offenbach	General de Brabant
N. Rimsky-Korsakov	Flight of the Bumble Bee
A. Utrera	Green Eyes
N. Mendez	

Title	Adapter/Lyricist
GREENER PASTURES	C. Warnick
	C. Leigh
GREETING TO SPRING	R. Atzler
GRIEF	G. Woodworth
	B. Cursch
GRIEG'S CONCERTO MARCH	D. Jacobs
LES GRISETTES DE PARIS	M. Pahl
	V. Leon
	C. Warnick
	L. Stein
GROGH	ballet
GUARDA CHE LUNA	G. Malgoni
"THE GUIDING LIGHT" THEME	unlisted
A GUY IS A GUY	O. Brand
GYPSY DANCE	A. Goodman
GYPSY RHAPSODY	H. Grant
GYPSY RONDO	various
GYPSY TRIO	unlisted
GYPSY'S LIBERTY	G. Hinrichs
HABANERA HOE DOWN	A. Russell
	H. Meilhac
	L. Halevy
HAFFNER SYMPHONY	unlisted
HAIL COLUMBIA	J. Hopkinson
HAIL, HAIL, THE GANG'S ALL HERE	various
THE HALL OF THE SWINGIN' KING	L. Brown
	J. Hill

Composer	Source
R. Schumann	Traumerei
J. Strauss	Blue Danube Waltz
A. Dvorak	unlisted
E. Grieg	Piano Concerto in a
F. Lehar	The Merry Widow
A. Copland	Dance Symphony
L. Beethoven	Sonata for Piano 14
unlisted	Aphrodite
d'Yrfey	A Knave Is a Knave
N. Rimsky-Korsakov	Capriccio Espagnole
F. Liszt	Dance Hongroise
J. Haydn	Trio 5 in G
J. Haydn	Trio 5 in G
A. Dvorak	Gypsy Song
G. Bizet	Carmen (Habañera)
W. Mozart	Symphony 35 in D (K. 385)
P. Phile	The Washington March
A. Sullivan	The Pirates of Penzance
E. Grieg	Peer Gynt (Hall of the Mountain King)

51

Title	Adapter/Lyricist
HAMBURGER SONATA	unlisted
HAND IN HAND	R. Wright
	G. Forrest
THE HAPPIEST GIRL IN THE WORLD	E. Harburg
HARK, HARK THE LARK	A. Ross
THE HARP OF THE POET	unlisted
THE HARPSICHORD PLAYER	W. Rolfe
HARVEY AND SHEILA	A. Sherman
HAT SHOP	M. Pahl
	C. Warnick
	I. Kostal
HAUNTING HUMORESQUE	F. Black
HAYDN SEEKS	L. Singer
	S. Marlowe
HEADACHES	A. Sherman
HEART DIVINE	E. Lorenz
HEBREW RHAPSODY	unlisted
HELLO MUDDAH, HELLO FADDAH	A. Sherman
THE HEN SYMPHONY	unlisted
HERE	H. Grant
	D. Cochran
HERE AND NOW	G. Benson
	H. Meilhac
HERE BEAUTY DWELLS	G. Galina
	G. Farrar
HE'S A JOLLY GOOD FELLOW	traditional

Composer	Source
C. P. E. Bach	Sonata for Flute and Piano in G
S. Rachmaninoff	Suite for Two Pianos 3 (Romance)
J. Offenbach	La Périchole
F. Schubert	Nachtigall
F. Mendelssohn	Piano Piece in E (Op. 38, #3)
W. Mozart	Sonata 3 in C (K. 545)
traditional (Hebrew)	Have Nagila
J. Strauss	unlisted
A. Dvorak	Humoresque
J. Haydn	Sonata in D
A. Hoffman	Heartaches
A. Dvorak	Symphony 9 (New World)
E. Bloch	Schelomo
A. Ponchielli	La Gioconda (Dance of the Hours)
J. Haydn	Symphony 83 in g
G. Verdi	Rigoletto (Caro Nome)
G. Bizet	Carmen
S. Rachmaninoff	Song (Op. 21, #7)
L. Beethoven	Wellington's Victory

Title	Adapter/Lyricist
HE'S IN LOVE	R. Wright
	G. Forrest
HEY DERRY DOWN DERRY	H. Baker
HI, FOLKS, WHAT'S NEW?	M. Pahl
	C. Warnick
	E. Eager
	I. Kostal
"HIGHWAY PATROL" THEME	unlisted
HILL OF DREAMS	R. Wright
	G. Forrest
"HILLTOP HOUSE" THEME	unlisted
HIS WORLD SHALL STAND	E. Tollotson
HO JOLLY JENKINS	J. Sturgis
HOLD MY HAND, GIOVANNI	G. Kingsley
HOLIDAY FOR STATES	A. Sherman
	L. Busch
HOLIDAY GREETING	H. Cykman
	W. Gilbert
	F. Moritt
"HOLLYWOOD HOTEL" THEME	L. Hart
HOLY ART THOU	various
HOME TO OUR MOUNTAIN	S. Cammerand
	C. Jeffereys
HOMELESS	C. von Sternberg
HOMESVILLE	B. Homer
HOMEWARD	G. Borch
HOMEWARD	R. Wright
	G. Forrest
HOMEWARD TO YOU	R. Bennett

Composer	Source
A. Borodin	Prince Igor (Polovtsian Dances)
J. Bach	Cantata
J. Strauss	unlisted
R. Llewellyn	Highway Patrol Theme
E. Grieg	Piano Concerto in a
J. Brahms	Cradle Song
J. Sibelius	Finlandia
A. Sullivan	Ivanhoe
W. Mozart	Don Giovanni (La ci darem la mano)
D. Rose	Holiday for Strings
F. Mendelssohn	unlisted
R. Rodgers	Blue Moon
G. Handel	Xerxes (Largo)
G. Verdi	Il Trovatore
F. Mendelssohn	unlisted
A. Dvorak	Symphony 9
E. Grieg	unlisted
S. Rachmaninoff	Prelude in g (Op. 23)
E. Coates	unlisted

55

Title	Adapter/Lyricist
HOMEWARD VOYAGE	S. Jacobson
HOP HOP HOP	J. Besler
	A. Welte
HOP UP	A. Sundgaard
HORNPIPE CONCERTO	unlisted
HOT BARCAROLLE	J. Barbier
	A. Stordahl
	M. Wolfson
THE HOT CANARY	F. Zabach
HOT DIGGETY	D. Manning
	A. Hoffman
HOW BLEST ARE THEY	W. Birbeck
	A. Davidson
HOW BRIGHT THE STARS	R. Noble
HOW CAN I TELL YOU	I. Taylor
	H. Stanley
HOW DO YOU DO?	unlisted
HOW LIKE UNTO A FLOWER	N. Cain
HOW LONG WILT THOU FORGET ME?	R. Peery
	E. McNaughton
HOW LOVELY ARE THOU DWELLINGS	H. Chambers
HOW LOVELY IS THY DWELLING PLACE	various
HOW SHOULD I YOUR TRUE LOVE KNOW?	W. Shakespeare
	L. Tieck
HOW SOON, OH MOON?	E. Harburg
HOW STRANGE	E. Grant
	G. Kahn
	H. Stothart

56

Composer	Source
E. Grieg	unlisted
E. Humperdinck	Hansel and Gretel
K. Weill	unlisted
G. Handel	Concerto Grosso 7
J. Offenbach	Tales of Hoffman (Barcarole)
F. Poliakin	Le Canari
E. Chabrier	España
P. Tchaikovsky	unlisted
R. Noble	Indian Suite
E. Grieg	Piano Concerto in a
J. Haydn	String Quartet in G (Op. 33, #5)
R. Schumann	Du Bist wie eine Blume
P. Tchaikovsky	None But the Lonely Heart
J. Brahms	Requiem
J. Brahms	Requiem
J. Brahms	unlisted
J. Offenbach	Orpheus in Hades
B. Prozorovsky	Kak Stranno

Title	Adapter/Lyricist
HOW STRANGE A MOOD IS MINE	J. Sonneleithner
	T. Baker
HUMORESCAPADE	T. Mottola
HUMORESQUE NOVELTY	A. Goodman
HUMOROUS HUMORESQUE	S. Henderson
HUNGARIAN GOULASH #5	A. Sherman
HUNGARIAN MARCH	various
HUNGARIAN RONDO	F. Kreisler
THE HUNT	unlisted
THE HUNT	unlisted
THE HUNT QUARTET	unlisted
THE HUNT SYMPHONY	unlisted
HUNTING SONG	unlisted
HUNT'S GOULASH	V. Alexander
HUNTING CHORUS	F. King
	N. MacFarren
	T. Baker
HUP TWO THREE	E. Harburg
	J. Gorney
	R. de Cormier
HURRAH FOR PAREE	J. Barbier
	M. Pahl
	C. Warnick
HURRIED TENSION	W. Hauenschild
HURRY	R. Hildreth
HUT OF BABA YAGA	various

Composer	Source
L. Beethoven	unlisted
A. Dvorak	Humoresque
A. Dvorak	Humoresque
A. Dvorak	Humoresque
J. Brahms	Hungarian Dance 5
H. Berlioz	Damnation of Faust
J. Haydn	unlisted
L. Beethoven	Sonata for Piano 18 in E flat (Op. 31)
N. Paganini	Caprice 9 in E
J. Haydn	String Quartet in B flat
J. Haydn	Symphony 72 in D
F. Mendelssohn	Piano Piece in A (Op. 19, #3)
J. Brahms	Hungarian Dance 5
C. Weber	Der Freischütz
J. Offenbach	unlisted
J. Offenbach	Tales of Hoffman
F. Schubert	Symphony 8
R. Schumann	Sonata in d
M. Mussorgsky	Pictures at an Exhibition

Title	Adapter/Lyricist
HYMN OF BETROTHAL	R. Wright
	G. Forrest
HYMN OF PRAISE	unlisted
HYMN TO JOY	H. van Dyke
HYMN TO NIGHT	M. Spicker
	T. Taker
HYMN TO THE ETERNAL	L. Saar
	F. Schiller
	A. Kilburn
HYMN TO THE SUN	various
HYMN TO VENUS	J. Mayhall
	L. Murray
I AM FREE	H. Simeone
	V. Leon
I BELIEVE IN ONE GOD	A. Henderson
I CAN'T FIND MY WIFE	R. Martin
	T. Martin
	F. Zell
	R. Genee
I CAN'T DANCE	A. Sherman
	L. Busch
I CAN'T REMEMBER	C. Lampl
	M. Jaffe
I CATCH THE BIRDS FROM DAWN TO DARK	R. Martin
	T. Martin
I FOUND MY LOVE	A. Szirmai
	A. Robinson
	P. Knepler
	C. Cummer
	E. Gilbert

Composer	Source
E. Grieg	To Spring
F. Mendelssohn	Symphony 2
L. Beethoven	Symphony 9
L. Beethoven	unlisted
F. Schubert	unlisted
N. Rimsky-Korsakov	Le Coq d'Or
R. Wagner	Tannhäuser
F. Lehar	The Merry Widow
P. Tchaikovsky	Russian church service
J. Strauss	A Night in Venice
E. Grieg	Norwegian Dance 2
E. Granados	Spanish Dance
W. A. Mozart	The Magic Flute
J. Strauss, Jr.	Three Waltzes

Title	Adapter/Lyricist
I FOUND YOU IN THE RAIN	unlisted
I GET IDEAS	D. Cochran
I GO MY WAY	C. Warnick C. Leigh
I GUESS I'LL HAVE TO GO ON DREAMING	D. Bernier
I HATE THE WALTZ	C. Warnick M. Pahl R. Genee C. Leigh C. Hoffman
I KNOW I LOVE YOU	J. Klenner
I LIKE BACH	F. Loffler
I LIKE TO LOVE YOU	I. Schnitzer R. Martin T. Martin
I LOOK AT HEAVEN	B. Austin E. Martin
I LOOKED FOR YOU	J. Torre F. Spielman
I LOST MY SHIRT	I. Berlin
"I LOVE A MYSTERY" THEME	unlisted
I LOVED MY LOVE	E. Maschwitz B. Grun
I LOVE YOU	R. Wright G. Forrest
I MEAN TO SAY I LOVE YOU	O. Hammerstein I
I NEVER DREAMED OF SUCH A THING	M. Pahl C. Warnick I. Kostal

Composer	Source
F. Chopin	Prelude 7 in A
I. Sanders	Adios Muchachos
R. Schumann	unlisted
P. Tchaikovsky	Nutcracker Suite
J. Strauss	unlisted
F. Chopin	Nocturne 2 (Op. 9)
J. S. Bach	Well-Tempered Clavier 1 (Prelude 9)
J. Strauss	The Gypsy Baron
E. Grieg	Piano Concerto in a
P. Tchaikovsky	unlisted
G. Bizet	Carmen (Toreador Song)
J. Sibelius	Valse Triste
A. Dvorak	unlisted
E. Grieg	Ich Liebe Dich (Jeg Elsker Dig)
E. Korngold	unlisted
J. Strauss	unlisted

Title	Adapter/Lyricist
"I REMEMBER MAMA" THEME	unlisted
I SEE BONES	A. Sherman
I THINK OF YOU	J. Elliot
I WANT SO MUCH	M. Pahl C. Warnick E. Eager I. Kostal
I WANT SOME LOVIN'	L. Prima
I WANT TO BE NEAR YOU	unlisted
I WILL BRING YOU MUSIC	D. Broekman
I WONDER	G. Bruns W. Hibler T. Sears
I WONDER AS I WANDER	J. Latouche B. Kaper
I'D GIVE THE WORLD	M. Pahl C. Warnick I. Kostal
I'LL BE REMEMBERING	B. Grun E. Maschwitz
I'LL NEVER COMPLAIN	various
I'M ALWAYS CHASING RAINBOWS	H. Carroll
I'M IN LOVE WITH ME	C. Warnick C. Leigh
I'M IN LOVE WITH VIENNA	E. Korngold
IF THIS IS GOODBYE	R. Wright G. Forrest

64

Composer	Source
G. Marie	La Cinquantine
unlisted	C'est Si Bon
S. Rachmaninoff	Piano Concerto 2 in c
J. Strauss	unlisted
P. Tchaikovsky	unlisted
Traditional (France)	Après de ma Blonde
S. Rachmaninoff	Piano Concerto 2 in c
P. Tchaikovsky	Sleeping Beauty (Waltz)
F. Chopin	Fantasie Impromptu 4 in c Sharp
J. Strauss	unlisted
A. Dvorak	Slavonic Dance 4 in F
R. Schumann	Ich grolle nicht
F. Chopin	Fantasie Impromptu in c Sharp
R. Schumann	unlisted
J. Strauss	unlisted
S. Rachmaninoff	Piano Concerto 2

Title	Adapter/Lyricist
IF YOU ARE BUT A DREAM	M. Jaffe
	N. Bonx
	J. Fulton
	B. Rubenstein
IF YOU DIG ME	B. Kessel
	H. Meilhac
IF YOU WERE MINE	A. Previn
	W. Katz
ILLUMINATIONS	ballet
IMMORTAL SONG	S. Gaines
AN IMPERIAL CONFERENCE	J. Latouche
IMPORTANT EVENT	M. Vagrich
AN IMPROVISATION ON CHOPIN	R. Coniff
IN AN 18TH CENTURY DRAWING ROOM	unlisted
IN AUTUMN	T. Baker
	A. Dorffel
IN DREAMS	H. Brana
	S. Sinkler
IN GOD'S GREAT LOVE	F. Rogers
IN LONDON TOWN	unlisted
IN SPRING	W. Sharpless
	B. Kaye
IN SUMMER FIELDS	unlisted
IN THE BASTILLE	M. Pahl
	C. Warnick
	E. Eager
	I. Kostal
IN THE COURT OF KUBLA KHAN	M. Pahl
	C. Warnick
	I. Kostal

Composer	Source
A. Rubenstein	Romance in E flat
G. Bizet	Carmen
A. Rubenstein	unlisted
B. Britten	Les Illuminations
P. Tchaikovsky	Song
F. Chopin	Etude 5 in G flat
R. Schumann	unlisted
F. Chopin	Nocturne 2 in E flat
W. A. Mozart	Sonata for Piano 15 in C (K. 545)
F. Mendelssohn	unlisted
J. Brahms	unlisted
R. Schumann	Die Lotosblume (Op. 25 #7)
E. Elgar	Cockaigne Overture
F. Mendelssohn	Piano Piece in A (Op. 62, #6)
J. Brahms	Mondenschein (Op. 86 #2)
J. Strauss	unlisted
N. Rimsky-Korsakov	unlisted

Title	Adapter/Lyricist
IN THE GARDEN	various
IN THE HALL OF THE MOUNTAIN KING CHA CHA CHA	V. Lopez
IN THE HUSH OF THE NIGHT	J. Davis
IN THE MOON MIST	J. Lawrence
IN THE SILENCE OF THE NIGHT	various
IN YOUR ARMS	J. Melis
IN YOUR MOONLIT BOWER	unlisted
INDIAN SUITE	unlisted
INTO THE NIGHT	G. Lessner R. Sour
IS IT YOU	E. Eager
THE ISLE OF MAY	A. Kostalanetz
IT MUSTN'T HAPPEN NOW	M. Pahl C. Warnick E. Eager I. Kostal
ITALIAN CONCERTO	unlisted
ITALIAN SYMPHONY	unlisted
IT'S ALL IN THE GAME	C. Sigman
IT'S GRIEG TO ME	B. Shefter
IT'S NO SECRET THAT I LOVE YOU	A. Stillman
IT'S NUMBER FOUR	M. Wilson
I'VE ALWAYS LOVED YOU	L. Flato
"I'VE GOT A SECRET" THEME	unlisted

68

Composer	Source
C. Goldmark	Symphony 1
E. Grieg	Peer Gynt
N. Rimsky-Korsakov	Scheherazade
P. Goddard	Melody
S. Rachmaninoff	In The Silent Night (Op. 4#3)
P. Tchaikovsky	unlisted
A. Dvorak	Humoresque
E. MacDowell	Suite 2 in e (Op. 48)
J. Strauss	unlisted
N. Rimsky-Korsakov	Scheherazade
P. Tchaikovsky	Quartet in D (Andante Cantabile)
J. Strauss	unlisted
J. S. Bach	Concerto in F
F. Mendelssohn	Symphony 4
C. Dawes	Melody
E. Grieg	unlisted
E. Lecuona	Damisela Encantadora
L. Beethoven	unlisted
S. Rachmaninoff	unlisted
L. Anderson	Plink, Plank, Plunk

Title	Adapter/Lyricist
IVY ROSE	A. Hoffman D. Manning
"THE JACK BENNY PROGRAM" THEME	L. Robin
JARDIN AUX LILAS	ballet
THE JAZZ MIKADO	W. Gilbert M. Liebman
JENA SYMPHONY	unlisted
JIG	various
"JOHN'S OTHER WIFE" THEME	unlisted
THE JOKE	unlisted
"JOYCE JORDAN" THEME	unlisted
JOYFUL, JOYFUL, WE ADORE THEE	H. Sanders H. Van Dyke
JOYOUS PEASANT	unlisted
JUANITA BANANA	unlisted
JUBILATION WALTZ	C. Roberts
THE JUDGMENT OF PARIS	ballet
JULIET'S FAREWELL	G. Farrar
JUNE BARCAROLLE	A. Lange
JUNGLE DRUMS	C. O'Flynn C. Lombardo
JUPITER SYMPHONY	unlisted

Composer	Source
traditional	Russian folk song
R. Rainger	Love in Bloom
E. Chausson	Poème for Violin and Orchestra
A. Sullivan	The Mikado
L. Beethoven	Symphony in C
H. Purcell	The Gordian Knot Untied
R. Stultz	The Sweetest Story Ever Told
J. Haydn	String Quartet in E flat (Op. 33, #2)
Z. Fibich	Poème
L. Beethoven	Symphony 9
F. Mendelssohn	Piano Piece in A (Op. 102, #5)
G. Verdi	Caro Nome (Rigoletto)
E. Humperdinck	Hansel and Gretel
K. Weill	The Threepenny Opera
P. Tchaikovsky	Romeo and Juliet
P. Tchaikovsky	The Months
E. Lecuona	Canto Karaboli
W. A. Mozart	Symphony 41 in C (K. 551)

Title	Adapter/Lyricist
JUST A CONNOISSEUR	W. Hanighen
	J. Blackton
JUST A DREAM AGO	unlisted
JUST A LITTLE RING	H. Clutsam
	H. Reichert
	A. Ropes
	A. Willner
JUST AROUND THE CORNER	E. Maschwitz
	B. Grun
JUST FOR TONIGHT	J. Latouche
	B. Kaper
"JUST PLAIN BILL" THEME	unlisted
JUST SAY I LOVE HER	J. Dale
	E. Fusco
	M. Kalmanoff
	J. Val
	S. Ward
KEY TO THE KINGDOM	C. Sigman
THE KEY TO YOUR HEART	A. Stillman
KICKIN' THE CAN	D. Raye
KING COTTON	J. P. Sousa
KING OF THE MOUNTAIN	M. Gold
THE KISS	F. La Forge
	W. Earhart
THE KISS IN YOUR EYES	F. Kreisler
	J. Burke
KISS ME CARMEN	G. Sonneborn
KISS ME TONIGHT	F. Steininger
	F. Brown

Composer	Source
O. Straus	The Chocolate Soldier
G. Puccini	Madama Butterfly (Un Bel Di)
F. Schubert	unlisted
A. Dvorak	unlisted
F. Chopin	Etude 3 in E
traditional	Polly Wolly Doodle
R. Falvo	Dicitencello Vuie
A. Semprini	Mediterranean Concerto
M. Arnold	The Key (film theme)
J. Offenbach	unlisted
G. Verdi	Aida
E. Grieg	Peer Gynt (Hall of the Mountain King)
L. Beethoven	unlisted
R. Heuburger	The Opera Ball
G. Bizet	Carmen
P. Tchaikovsky	Song Without Words

Title	Adapter/Lyricist
KISS OF FIRE	L. Allen
	R. Hill
"KITTY KEENE" THEME	unlisted
KNOCKED-OUT NIGHTINGALE	B. Merrill
KRAFT MUSIC HALL	
see "THE BING CROSBY SHOW"	
KREUTZER SONATA	unlisted
THE LADY AND THE FOOL	ballet
LALITA	J. Colonna
LAMENT	H. Meilhac
	G. Woodworth
THE LAMP IS LOW	M. Parish
LAND OF LOVE	R. Carlyle
	M. Caranda
	J. Washabaugh
LARGO	traditional
THE LARK QUARTET	unlisted
THE LAST ROSE OF SUMMER	T. Moore
LAST THOUGHT	unlisted
THE LAST WALTZ	J. Klenner
LAST COOL CLOWN	unlisted
LAUGHING SONG	various
LAUGHTER IS THE THING	C. Warnick
	M. Pahl
LAZY MARY	L. Monte

Composer	Source
A. Villoldo	El Choclo
P. Tchaikovsky	None But the Lonely Heart
F. Mendelssohn	unlisted
L. Beethoven	Sonata for Violin 9 in A
G. Verdi	themes
F. Schubert	Symphony 8
J. Offenbach	La Belle Hélène
M. Ravel	Pavan for a Dead Princess
J. Offenbach	unlisted
G. Handel	Xerxes (Ombra mai Fu)
J. Haydn	String Quartet in D (Op. 64, #5)
F. Flotow	Martha
L. Beethoven	Piano Piece in B flat
F. Chopin	Waltz 2 (Op. 64)
R. Leoncavallo	Pagliacci (Vesti le Giubba
J. Strauss	Die Fledermaus
J. Strauss	unlisted
P. Citorello	Luna Mezze Mare

Title	Adapter/Lyricist
LEBEN SIE WOHL	R. Wright G. Forrest
THE LEGEND OF VILIA	M. Pahl C. Warnick V. Leon L. Stein
LENINGRAD SYMPHONY	unlisted
LEPROSY	traditional
LESSONS IN LOVE	R. Bodansky H. Smith R. Smith A. Willner
LET ALL THINGS NOW LIVING	J. Cowley
LET SAINTS ON EARTH IN CONCERT SING	F. Butcher C. Wesley
LET YOUR HEART LEAD THE WAY	M. David J. Livingston A. Hoffman
THE LIDO	M. Pahl C. Warnick I. Kostal
LIFE IS A DREAM	A. Freed
"LIFE OF MARY SOTHERN" THEME	unlisted
"LIFE WITH LUIGI" THEME	unlisted
LIFT 'EM UP AND PUT 'EM DOWN	R. Bennett O. Hammerstein II H. Meilhac L. Halevy
LIKE HUNGARIAN	S. Phillips

76

Composer	Source
S. Rachmaninoff	Prelude 5 (Op. 23); Polichinelle 4 (Op. 3)
F. Lehar	Merry Widow (Vilia)
D. Schostakovich	Symphony 7
J. Gade	Jalousie
F. Lehar	Gypsy Lover
traditional (Welsh)	The Ash Grove
F. Mendelssohn	traditional
J. Brahms	unlisted
J. Strauss	unlisted
O. Straus	unlisted
H. von Tilzer	Just a Little Love, a Little Kiss
E. di Capua	Oh, Marie
G. Bizet	Carmen
F. Liszt	Hungarian Rhapsodies

Title	Adapter/Lyricist
LIKE NUTTY OVERTURE	M. Rogers
LIKE THERE'S NO PLACE LIKE	B. Kessell
	H. Meilhac
LILAC GARDEN	
see JARDIN AUX LILAS	
LILACS AND LOVE	unlisted
LINZ SYMPHONY	unlisted
LISA'S WALTZ	B. Leighton
	M. Wechsler
A LITTLE BOY AND A LITTLE	R. Wright
GIRL	G. Forrest
LITTLE BUTTERBALL	A. Sherman
	L. Busch
LITTLE FUGUE	unlisted
LITTLE HANDS	R. Wright
	G. Forrest
LITTLE JACK AND LITTLE JILL	unlisted
THE LITTLE MAGICIAN	J. Livingston
	C. Tobias
A LITTLE NIGHT JAZZ	G. Kingsley
LITTLE RUSSIAN SYMPHONY	unlisted
THE LITTLE SANDMAN	W. Stickles
	B. Brown
LITTLE SUITE	E. Irving
THE LITTLE THINGS WE LOVE	J. Klenner
LITTLE TRUMPET PIECE	unlisted

Composer	Source
P. Tchaikovsky	Nutcracker Suite
G. Bizet	Carmen
P. Tchaikovsky	Piano Concerto 1 in b flat
W. A. Mozart	Symphony 36 in C (K. 425)
G. Rossini	La Promessa
E. Grieg	Norwegian Dance in d
A. Sullivan	HMS Pinafore (Little Buttercup)
J. S. Bach	Fugue for Organ in g
S. Rachmaninoff	Vocalise 14 (Op. 34)
E. Grieg	Norwegian Dance 2
F. Schubert	Serenade
W. Mozart	Eine Kleine Nachtmusik
P. Tchaikovsky	Symphony 2 in c
J. Brahms	Sandmannchen
F. Mendelssohn	Songs Without Words
F. Chopin	Prelude 7 (Op. 28) and Minute Waltz
F. Mendelssohn	Scherzo in e

Title	Adapter/Lyricist
LIVE, LAUGH AND LOVE	W. Heymann R. Gilbert R. Leigh
LONDON SYMPHONY	unlisted
"THE LONE RANGER" THEME	unlisted
LONELY NIGHT	A. Wilder
LONESOME HEART	A. Ferrante L. Teicher
LONG MAY WE LOVE	C. Freedlin K. Goell I. Lane
LONGING	H. Berti S. Romberg H. Reichert D. Donnelly A. Willner
LOOK AT ME	unlisted
LOOK ME OVER ONCE	H. Dietz
THE LORD'S PRAYER	G. Dunham
THE LORD'S PRAYER	W. Wirges R. Maxwell
THE LORD'S PRAYER	R. Row
THE LORD'S PRAYER	W. Riegger A. Marlhorn
"LORENZO JONES" THEME	unlisted
"THE LORETTA YOUNG SHOW" THEME	unlisted
LOST HAPPINESS	unlisted
LOST ILLUSION	unlisted

80

Composer	Source
J. Strauss	unlisted
R. Vaughan Williams	Symphony 2
G. Rossini	William Tell (Overture)
A. Jahrnfelt	Berceuse
P. Tchaikovsky	unlisted
P. Tchaikovsky	Symphony 5
F. Schubert	unlisted
S. de Fuentes	Miriame Asi
J. Strauss	Die Fledermaus
P. Tchaikovsky	Russian Church Service
G. Handel	traditional
J. Sibelius	traditional
C. Franck	traditional
L. Denza	Funiculi, Funicula
H. Lubin B. Craig	Dear Loretta
F. Mendelssohn	Piano Piece in c (Op. 38, #2)
F. Mendelssohn	Piano Piece in f Sharp (Op. 67, #1)

Title	Adapter/Lyricist
LOST IN A DREAM	C. Warnick
	M. Liebman
LOTSA LUCK	A. Sherman
	L. Busch
THE LOUVRE	M. Pahl
	C. Warnick
	I. Kostal
LOVE ALONE	D. Carter
LOVE AND WINE	A. Ross
LOVE AND WINE	J. Limbacher
LOVE AT LAST	E. Korngold
	H. Baker
LOVE COMES EASY TO ME	A. Ronnell
LOVE GOODBYE	A. Ross
LOVE IN MY HEART	various
LOVE IS A LOVELY ILLUSION	A. Stillman
	W. Irwin
LOVE IS A PILGRIM	G. MacDonough
LOVE IS LIKE THE ROSE	H. Smith
	R. Smith
LOVE MAKES THE WORLD GO ROUND	D. Cochran
LOVE ME TENDER	E. Presley
LOVE SINGS A LULLABY	unlisted
LOVE STAR	P. Lewis
	V. Rose
	L. Stock
A LOVE STORY	T. Mossman

Composer	Source
J. Strauss	unlisted
V. Herbert	unlisted
J. Strauss	unlisted
J. Strauss	unlisted
F. Lehar	Gypsy Love
J. Strauss	Die Fledermaus (Du and Du)
J. Offenbach	La Belle Helene
O. Straus	unlisted
F. Lehar	The Count of Luxembourg
F. Lehar	The Merry Widow
F. Liszt	Les Preludes
F. Lehar	unlisted
F. Lehar	Gypsy Love
O. Straus	La Ronde
S. Foster	Aura Lee
B. Godard	Berceuse
H. Wieniawski	Concerto in d
R. Schumann	Piano Concerto in a

Title	Adapter/Lyricist
LOVE WILL FIND YOU	A. Sirmay
	D. Carter
LOVE WILL KEEP US YOUNG	E. Leslie
LOVE'S ROUNDABOUT	J. Purcell
	P. Ducre
LOVE-SICK SERENADE	E. Harburg
THE LOVELIEST NIGHT OF THE YEAR	I. Aaronson
	P. Webster
LOVERS BY STARLIGHT	D. Costa
	A. Ferrante
	L. Teicher
LOVER'S CONCERTO	unlisted
LOVERS IN PARADISE	A. Ferrante
	L. Teicher
LOVE'S OWN WALTZ	E. Conrad
	R. Braine
LULLABY FOR WOLFGANG	G. Kingsley
LULLABY OF BACHLAND	F. Loffler
LULLABY OF LOVE	P. Webster
	G. Cates
LULLABY OF THE FIREBIRD	R. Forberg
LULLABY RUSSE	T. Charles
MADEMOISELLE LA BELLE ARLESIENNE	G. Sonneborn
MADRID, WHERE IS MY LOVE	N. Cole
	J. Lange
	H. Meilhac
MAGIC IS THE MOONLIGHT	C. Pasquale
THE MAGIC NUTCRACKER	J. Kerley

Composer	Source
J. Strauss	The Great Waltz
J. Brahms	Waltz in A flat
O. Straus	Waltz Dream
J. Offenbach	La Belle Hélène
J. Rosas	Over the Waves
P. Tchaikovsky	Symphony 5
F. Chopin	Etude
A. Borodin	Prince Igor (Polovtsian Dances)
P. Tchaikovsky	Sleeping Beauty (Waltz)
W. Mozart	Piano Sonata 11 in A
J. S. Bach	Gib dich zufrieden und sei Stille
J. Brahms	Cradle Song
I. Stravinsky	Firebird Suite
A. Khatchaturian	Gayne (Lullaby)
G. Bizet	L'Arlesienne Suite
G. Bizet	Carmen
traditional (Spain)	Te Quiero Dijiste
P. Tchaikovsky	Nutcracker Suite

Title	Adapter/Lyricist
MAGIC OF MOONLIGHT AND LOVE	K. Hajos
	H. Smith
MAGIC OF YOUR LOVE	G. Kahn
	C. Grey
MAGIC WALTZ	V. Leon
	M. Pahl
	V. Stein
	C. Warnick
MAGICAL MORN	P. Weston
	O. Nash
MAKE LOVE TO ME	G. Brunies
	L. Koppolo
	P. Mares
	B. Pollack
	M. Stitzel
MAMBO DIABLO	H. Katz
	M. Dunby
MAMMY'S LULLABY	C. Spross
	E. Nowland
MARCH	P. Gallico
MARCH OF THE SUGAR PLUMMERS	E. Ballantine
MARCH OF THE TROLLGERS	R. Wright
	G. Forest
MARCHE ALLA TURCA see TURKISH MARCH	
MARCHETA	V. Schertzinger
MARGUERITA WALTZ	P. Henneberg
MARIA MY OWN	L. Gilbert

Composer	Source
P. Tchaikovsky	unlisted
F. Lehar	Lalalaika
F. Lehar	The Merry Widow
S. Prokofiev	Peter and the Wolf
A. Copeland W. Melrose W. Norvas	Tin Roof Blues
C. Saint-Saens	unlisted
A. Dvorak	Humoresque
F. Schubert	Divertissment a la Hongroise
P. Tchaikovsky	Nutcracker Suite
E. Grieg	Peer Gynt (Mountaineer's Song and March of the Dwarfs
O. Nicolai	The Merry Wives of Windsor
C. Gounod	Faust
E. Lecuona	Maria La O

Title	Adapter/Lyricist
MARIA THERESA	unlisted
MARKET DAY	M. Pahl
	C. Warnick
	C. Huxley
	E. Eager
THE MARKSMAN	C. Godfrey
MARTHA MARTHA	L. Clinton
	C. Boswell
MARTHA MARTHA CHA CHA CHA	H. Harden
"MARTIN KANE" THEME	unlisted
MARVELOUS CAR	N. Luboff
	E. Brown
"MARY MARLIN" THEME	unlisted
MARY NOBLE, BACKSTAGE WIFE see "BACKSTAGE WIFE"	
MARYLAND, MY MARYLAND	J. Randall
MASSA DEAR	H. Loomis
	F. Manley
"MATINEE THEATER" THEME	unlisted
MATRIMONY	H. Smith
	R. Smith
MAXIM'S	M. Pahl
	R. Wright
	V. Leon
	L. Stein
"MAXWELL HOUSE COFFEE TIME" THEME	M. Wilson
MAY BREEZES	unlisted
MAYHEM IN STRAUSS	S. Kuller
MEADOWLAND	H. Rome

Composer	Source
J. Haydn	Symphony 48 in C
N. Rimsky-Korsakov	unlisted
E. Elgar	Three Bavarian Dances
F. Flotow	Martha (M'Appari)
F. Flotow	Martha (M'Appari)
R. Llewellyn	Martin Kane Theme
G. Verdi	unlisted
C. Debussy	Clair de Lune
traditional	Oh, Tannenbaum
A. Dvorak	Symphony 9 (New World)
E. Truman	Matinee Theater Theme
F. Lehar	Gypsy Love
F. Lehar	The Merry Widow
M. Wilson	You and I
F. Mendelssohn	Piano Piece in G (Op. 62, #1)
J. Strauss	unlisted
traditional (Russia)	Cavalry of the Steppes

Title	Adapter/Lyricist
MEADOW LARK	J. Latouche
	B. Kaper
MERCURY SYMPHONY	unlisted
METAMORPHOSES	ballet
MIDNIGHT BELLS	unlisted
MIDSUMMER'S EVE	R. Wright
	G. Forrest
MILE A MINUTE WALTZ	H. Beau
	D. Harris
MILLI'S WEDDING	E. Maschwitz
	B. Grun
MINKA	W. Guidry
	J. Niles
	C. Ramsay
MINUET IN MAMBO	J. August
MINUET IN 4	G. Kingsley
MINUET TO LET	B. Homer
MINUTE WALTZ	unlisted
MINUTES WITH MAGNANTE	C. Magnante
"MR. AND MRS. NORTH" THEME	unlisted
"MR, KEEN, TRACER OF LOST PERSONS" THEME	unlisted
MISTER TAPTOE	unlisted
MISTY DAYS, LOVELY NIGHTS	R. Lewis
MOE ZART'S TURKEY TROT	C. Carling
	J. Washburne

Composer	Source
F. Chopin	Mazurka 5 in B flat
J. Haydn	Symphony 43
P. Hindemith	Symphonic Metamorphoses on a theme by Weber
R. Heuburger	The Opera Ball (Separate Room)
E. Grieg	Scherzo in e and 'Twas a Lovely Eve in June
F. Chopin	Waltz 6
A. Dvorak	unlisted
traditional	Ukranian Folk song
I. Paderewski	Minuet in G
W. Mozart	Divertmento 17 in D
J. Haydn	unlisted
F. Chopin	Waltz 6 in D (Op. 64)
F. Chopin	Waltz 6
J. Kern	The Way You Look Tonight
N. Coward	Someday I'll Find You
traditional (Creole)	M'sieu Banjo
S. Rachmaninoff	Vocalise
W. Mozart	Rondo alla Turca

Title	Adapter/Lyricist
MONA LISA	M. Pahl
	C. Warnick
	E. Eager
	I. Kostal
MOON LOVE	M. David
	A. Kostelanetz
"MOON RIVER" THEME	unlisted
MOONLIGHT AND ROSES	C. Daniels
	B. Black
MOONLIGHT AND ROSES	unlisted
MOONLIGHT LOVE	D. Savino
	M. Parish
MOONLIGHT MADNESS	J. Wisner
MOONLIGHT MADONNA	W. Scotti
	P. Webster
MOONLIGHT MASQUERADE	T. Camarata
	J. Lawrence
THE MOONLIGHT MINUET	J. Klenner
MOONLIGHT ON THE WATER	P. Mondrone
	J. Crawford
MOONLIGHT SOLILOQUY	J. Latouche
	B. Kaper
MOONLIGHT SONATA	unlisted
THE MOOR'S PAVAN	ballet
MORE	N. Newell
MORE THAN ANYTHING	unlisted
MORNING	M. Janow
	L. Esbeer
	G. Farrar

Composer	Source
J. Strauss	unlisted
P. Tchaikovsky	Symphony 5 (Andante Cantabile)
C. Debussy	Clair de Lune
E. La Mare	Organ Andantino in D flat
Z. Fibich	Cathedral Meditation
C. Debussy	Clair de Lune
L. Beethoven	Piano Sonata 14
Z. Fibich	Poème
I. Albeniz	Tango in D
F. Chopin	Minuets 1 and 3 (Op. 70)
G. Rossini	unlisted
F. Chopin	Nocturne 5 in F Sharp
L. Beethoven	Sonata for Piano 14 in c Sharp (Op. 27)
H. Purcell	The Gordian Knot Untied
R. Ortolani	Mondo Cane (film theme)
P. Tchaikovsky	Swan Lake
S. Rachmaninoff	unlisted

Title	Adapter/Lyricist
MORNING, NOON AND NIGHT	unlisted
MORNING PRAYER	M. Carroll
	S. King
MORNING SONG	unlisted
MORNING SONG	T. Baker
	A. Dorfell
MOTHER'S LAMENT	I. Taylor
MOUNTAIN KINGERY	L. Garisto
	J. Wolf
	H. Moss
MOZART GOES FORTY	P. Burgett
MOZART MEANDERS	L. Singer
MOZART'S TURKISH TROTT	E. Lawrence
MURPHY'S PIG	E. Maschwitz
	B. Grun
MUSIC BOX	I. Taylor
	H. Stanley
MUSICAL CHAIRS	B. Leighton
	M. Wechsler
MY BLUE DANUBE	H. Frey
	H. Jackson
MY CONSOLATION	M. Stoloff
	H. Sukman
	N. Washington
MY COUSIN CARUS	G. Edward
	E. Madden
MY DARLING KAROLKA	E. Maschwitz
	B. Grun
MY DREAM OF LOVE	J. Melis
	E. Hubbard

Composer	Source
E. Toselli	Serenade
J. Sibelius	Finlandia
F. Mendelssohn	Piano Piece in G (Op. 62, #4)
F. Mendelssohn	unlisted
E. Grieg	Peer Gynt (Ase's Death)
E. Grieg	Peer Gynt (Hall of the Mountain King)
W. A. Mozart	Symphony 40
W. A. Mozart	unlisted
W. A. Mozart	Rondo alla Turca
A. Dvorak	unlisted
E. Grieg	unlisted
G. Verdi	Rigoletto
J. Strauss	Blue Danube Waltz
F. Liszt	Consolation
R. Leoncavallo	Pagliacci (Vesti la Giubba)
A. Dvorak	unlisted
F. Liszt	Liebesträum

Title	Adapter/Lyricist
MY DREAMS ARE ONLY DRIFTWOOD	unlisted
MY HEART SAYS YES	C. Warnick
	M. Liebman
MY HOPEFUL HEART	B. Raleigh
MY HYMN TO THE SUN	H. Ross
	H. Terry
MY JOE	O. Hammerstein I
MY JOHANN	various
MY LITTLE NEST OF HEAVENLY BLUE	H. Reichert
	S. Spaeth
	A. Willner
MY LOVE FOR YOU	B. Leighton
	M. Wechsler
MY LOVE FOR YOU	F. Schumann
MY LOVE LOVES ME	R. Evans
	J. Livingston
MY MOONLIGHT MADONNA see MOONLIGHT MADONNA	
MY OWN TRUE LOVE	M. David
MY PRAYER	J. Kennedy
MY REVERIE	L. Clinton
MY SONG FOR YOU	G. Griffin
MY SONG OF INDIA see SONG OF INDIA	
MY SWEETEST SONG OF ALL	
	H. Clutsam
"MY TRUE STORY" THEME	unlisted

Composer	Source
F. Chopin	Fantasie Impromptu
J. Strauss	unlisted
E. Lecuona	Yo Nada Puedo Hacer

N. Rimsky-
  Korsakov
	Le Coq d'Or (Hymn to
	  the Sun)

G. Bizet	Carmen (Micaela's Air)
E. Grieg	Norwegian Dance
F. Lehar	Frasquita (Serenade)
G. Puccini	La Boheme (Musetta's Waltz Song)
J. Brahms	Meine Liebe
J. Martin	Plasir d'Amour
M. Steiner	Gone With the Wind (Tara's Theme)
G. Boulanger	Avant de Mourir
C. Debussy	Reverie
L. Beethoven	Piano Sonata 14
F. Schubert	unlisted
C. Hathaway	My True Story

Title	Adapter/Lyricist
MY TWILIGHT DREAM	E. Duchin
	L. Sherwood
	R. Sherwood
MY ZELDA	A. Sherman
	L. Busch
"MYRT AND MARGE" THEME	R. Hubbeld
NADJA	G. Federlein
	F. Martens
NAIL IN THE HORSESHOE	J. Latouche
NAILA BOUNCE	A. Datz
"NATIONAL FARM AND HOME HOUR" THEME	unlisted
NATION'S PRAYER	G. Barr
NATURE'S PRAISE OF GOD	S. Spaeth
NEAR THE CROSS	I. Emerson
NEAR THE WALLS OF SEVILLA	L. Halevy
	A. Mathullath
	H. Meilhac
	J. Zamecnik
NEMRAC	R. Bloch
	H. Meilhac
NEVER BEDEVIL THE DEVIL	E. Harburg
	R. DeCormier
	J. Gorney
NEVER HAVE I SEEN A MAIDEN SO FAIR	D. O'Connor
	E. Maxwell
	S. Miller
	W. Scharf

Composer	Source
F. Chopin	Nocturne 2 in E flat
traditional	Matilda
J. Goeden	Poor Butterfly
A. Dvorak	
W. A. Mozart	Marriage of Figaro (Non più andrai)
L. Delibes	unlisted
J. P. Sousa	Stars and Stripes Forever
C. Franck	Panis Angelicus
L. Beethoven	
G. Rossini	Stabat Mater
G. Bizet	Carmen (Seguidilla)
G. Bizet	Carmen
J. Offenbach	Lischen et Frischen
F. Mendelssohn	unlisted

Title	Adapter/Lyricist
NEVER LET ME GO	J. Barbier
	M. Pahl
	C. Warnick
NEVER TRUST A VIRGIN	E. Harburg
NEVER YOUR LOVE	M. Berk
	B. Hays
	H. Parris
NEW WORLD JUMP	B. Sherwood
NEW WORLD ON ITS WAY	B. Treharne
	G. van Loon
NEW WORLD ROCK	unlisted
NEW WORLD SYMPHONY	unlisted
NIGHT OF MY NIGHTS	R. Wright
	G. Forrest
NIGHT WIND	F. Steinger
	F. Brown
NIGHTFALL	I. Wilson
NINA'S DANCE	B. Leighton
	M. Wechsler
NO GREATER LOVE	J. Diggs
	D. Savino
NO LOVE BUT YOUR LOVE	A. Schroeder
	W. Gold
NO ONE THANKS THE GO-BETWEEN	M. Pahl
	C. Warnick
	V. Leon
	S. Stein
	C. Leigh
NO ONE TOLD ME	E. Maschwitz
	B. Grun

Composer	Source
J. Offenbach	Tales of Hoffman
J. Offenbach	Orpheus in The Underworld (Can-Can 2)
F. Schubert	unlisted
A. Dvorak	Symphony 9 (New World)
A. Dvorak	Symphony 9 (New World)
A. Dvorak	Symphony 9 (New World)
A. Dvorak	Symphony 9 (New World)
A. Borodin	Serenade
P. Tchaikovsky	Song Without Words
F. Liszt	Liebesträum
V. Bellini	I Puritani
P. Tchaikovsky	Piano Concerto 1
R. Leoncavallo	Mattinata
F. Lehar	The Merry Widow
A. Dvorak	unlisted

Title	Adapter/Lyricist
NO OTHER LOVE	P. Weston
	R. S. Keith
NO OTHER LOVE	O. Hammerstein I]
NO PLACE LIKE ROME	unlisted
NO STAR IS LOST	F. Fisher
NO TIME	M. Holliday
THE NOOSE HANGS HIGH	S. Meyer
	E. Brandt
NOT SINCE NINEVAH	R. Wright
	G. Forrest
NOW	R. Wright
	G. Forrest
NOW AND FOREVER	J. Savitt
	A. Stillman
NOW HERE'S A SUMMER BREEZE	M. Willson
NOW I KNOW YOUR FACE BY HEART	J. Latouche
	B. Kaper
NOW IS MY MOMENT	R. Wright
	G. Forrest
NOW THERE, MR. RUBENSTEIN	R. Martin
NUTCRACKER SUITE GOES LATIN	D. Hyman
A NUTTY MARCHE	M. Rogers
O COME EVERYONE THAT THIRSTETH	E. Willoughby
O COME LET US WORSHIP	N. Norden
O FOR THE WINGS OF A DOVE	L. Dressler
	W. Bartholomew

Composer	Source
F. Chopin	Etude in E
R. Rodgers	Victory at Sea (theme)
P. Tchaikovsky	Capriccio Italien
P. Tchaikovsky	Symphony 6
F. Chopin	Waltz 1 in c Sharp
G. Verdi	unlisted
A. Borodin	Prince Igor (Polovtsian Dances)
E. Grieg	Waltz 2 and Violin Sonata 2
P. Tchaikovsky	Symphony 6 in b
L. Beethoven	unlisted
F. Chopin	Waltz in A flat
S. Rachmaninoff	Suite for Two Pianos (Waltz)
A. Rubenstein	Melody in F
P. Tchaikovsky	Nutcracker Suite
P. Tchaikovsky	Nutcracker Suite (March)
F. Mendelssohn	unlisted
P. Tchaikovsky	Russian church service
F. Mendelssohn	Hear My Prayer

Title	Adapter/Lyricist
O GOD OF LOVE	E. Korngold
	H. Meilhac
	L. Halevy
	A. Herbert
O, HEART OF MY COUNTRY	J. Latouche
	B. Kaper
O LAMB OF GOD MOST STAINLESS	P. Goetschius
O LOVELY NIGHT	M. Spicker
	J. Barbier
	M. Baum
O MORN OF BEAUTY	H. Matthews
O MY DEAR MARQUIS	A. Szirmai
	R. Simon
O NATIVE LAND	E. Ascher
O PRAISE HIM	M. Hokanson
	D. Benfield
O SINGING LAND	B. Treharne
	A. Griffin
THE OATH	E. Harburg
	R. DeCormier
	J. Gorney
OCTOBER SYMPHONY	unlisted
ODE TO A COOL GHOUL	A. Datz
OH BOY	A. Sherman
	L. Busch
OH, MR. BRAHMS	R. Linda
OH, THAT MITZIE	L. Robin
OH, THEODORA	traditional
OH, THOU WAVING FIELD OF GOLDEN GRAIN	A. Tolstoi
	G. Farrar

Composer	Source
J. Offenbach	La Belle Hélène
F. Chopin	Nocturne in E Flat
J. S. Bach	St. Matthew Passion
J. Offenbach	Barcarolle
J. Sibelius	Finlandia
J. Strauss	Die Fledermaus (Champagne Sec)
G. Verdi	Aida
J. S. Bach	Trumpet Suite
J. Sibelius	Finlandia
J. Offenbach	La Vie Parisienne
D. Shostakovich	Symphony 2
J. Massenet	unlisted
traditional	Mexican Hat Dance
J. Brahms	unlisted
O. Straus	unlisted
G. Bizet	Carmen (Toreador Song)
S. Rachmaninoff	unlisted

Title	Adapter/Lyricist
OH, WHAT A NIGHT	M. Pahl C. Warnick
AN OLD LOVE DIES	E. Eager H. Meilhac
OLD MACDONALD FARMS WITH BRAHMS	A. Templeton
OLD VIENNA	C. Warnick M. Pahl I. Kostal E. Eager L. Stein V. Leon
THE OLIVE TREE	R. Wright G. Forrest
ON GREAT LONE HILLS	G. Cates
ON SONG'S BRIGHT PINIONS	N. Page H. Heine
ON THAT DAY	R. Wright G. Forrest
ON THE ISLE OF MAY see THE ISLE OF MAY	
ON THE SHORE	unlisted
ONCE A YEAR IS NOT ENOUGH	E. Maschwitz B. Grun
ONCE AGAIN ROUND THE PARK	C. Warnick M. Pahl
ONCE IN A LIFETIME	unlisted
ONCE IN MAY	unlisted

Composer	Source
J. Strauss	Die Fledermaus
J. Offenbach	Orpheus in the Underworld
J. Brahms	unlisted
J. Strauss	Alt Wein
A. Borodin	Prince Igor (Love Duet)
J. Sibelius	Finlandia
F. Mendelssohn	On Wings of Song
S. Rachmaninoff	String Quartet in g; A Dream 5 (Op. 38)
F. Mendelssohn	Piano Piece in A flat (Op. 53)
A. Dvorak	unlisted
J. Strauss	unlisted
A. Thomas	Andante
T. M. Tobani	Hearts and Flowers

107

Title	Adapter/Lyricist
ONCE UPON A DREAM	G. Bruns
ONE BOY SENDS ME A ROSE	E. Maschwitz B. Grun
"ONE MAN'S FAMILY" THEME	unlisted
"ONE MAN'S FAMILY" THEME	unlisted
"THE O'NEILL'S" THEME	unlisted
ONLY ONCE	S. Allen B. Kendall
OPERA CHA CHA CHA	H. Harden F. Lemaire
ORCHESTRA IN A NUTCRACKER SHELL	R. Bennett
ORGAN SYMPHONY	unlisted
ORIENTAL CHA CHA CHA	H. Harden
OUDT COMES DER OOM PAH PAH	C. Warnick C. Leigh
"OUR GAL SUNDAY" THEME	unlisted
OUR LOVE	L. Clinton E. Emmerich B. Bernier
OUR SECRET RENDEZVOUS	unlisted
OUR SERENADE	W. Stein M. DeLugg
OUT FOR THE DAY	T. Phillips C. Lovett
OVER THE SUMMER SEA	F. Waller

Composer	Source
P. Tchaikovsky	Sleeping Beauty (Waltz)
A. Dvorak	unlisted
S. Barnes	Destiny Waltz
P. Carson	Patricia
traditional	Londonderry Air
E. de Curtis	Torna a Surriento
C. Saint-Saens	unlisted
P. Tchaikovsky	Nutcracker Suite
C. Saint-Saens	Symphony 3
N. Rimsky-Korsakov	Scheherazade
R. Schumann	The Happy Farmer
traditional	Red River Valley
P. Tchaikovsky	Romeo and Juliet (Overture)
J. Weinberger	Midnight Bells
F. Schubert	Serenade
F. Chopin	unlisted
G. Verdi	Rigoletto (La Donna e Mobile)

109

Title	Adapter/Lyricist
OVERSEAS	B. Weed
	C. Tyler
	H. Meilhac
	L. Halevy
OVERTURE FOR SHORTY	M. Rogers
OX MINUET	unlisted
OXFORD SYMPHONY	unlisted
PAD ON THE EDGE OF TOWN	B. Kessel
	H. Meilhac
PADDY'S MINUET	F. Novak
PAGAN NINNY KEEP-'ER-GOIN' STOMP	R. Ingle
PAGANINI AT A PARTY	R. Linda
PAGANINI IN RHYTHM	E. South
PAGANINI PLAYTIME	L. Stone
PAGANINI RHAPSODY	unlisted
PAGANINI VARIATIONS	unlisted
PANCHO THE PANTHER	O. Hammerstein I
	R. Bennett
	H. Meilhac
PAPER PAGLIACCI	G. Cines
PARADING IN THE PARK	J. Klenner
PARIS MARDI GRAS	I. Fields
PARIS SYMPHONY	unlisted
PARISIAN WAYS	M. Liebman
PARTNER COME AND DANCE WITH ME	R. Schmidt
	A. Welte

Composer	Source
J. Offenbach	unlisted
P. Tchaikovsky	Nutcracker Suite (Overture)
J. Haydn	Minuet for Orchestra
J. Haydn	Symphony 92
G. Bizet	Carmen
I. Paderewski	Minuet in G
N. Paganini	Perpetual Motion
N. Paganini	Perpetual Motion
N. Paganini	Perpetual Motion
N. Paganini	Perpetual Motion
S. Rachmaninoff	Rhapsody on a Theme of Paganini
J. Brahms	Variations on a Theme of Paganini
G. Bizet	Carmen
R. Leoncavallo	Pagliacci
F. Chopin	Polonaise 3 (Op. 40)
J. Offenbach	unlisted
W. A. Mozart	Symphony 31
F. Lehar	unlisted
E. Humperdinck	Hansel and Gretel

Title	Adapter/Lyricist
PAS DE DIX	ballet
PAS DE TROIS	ballet
"THE PASSING PARADE" THEME	unlisted
PASSION	unlisted
PASSION FLOWER	G. Garfield
	P. Botkin
	P. Murtagh
PASTORALE SYMPHONY	unlisted
PATHETIQUE SONATA	unlisted
PATHETIQUE SYMPHONY	unlisted
"PATRICE MUNSEL SHOW" THEME	unlisted
"PAUL WINCHELL SHOW" THEME	unlisted
PEANUT BRITTLE BRIGADE	D. Ellington
	B. Strayhorn
THE PEANUT VENDOR	W. Gilbert
	M. Sunshine
PEASANT CANTATA	unlisted
PEE WEE AND THE WOLF	V. Alexander
"PEPPER YOUNG'S FAMILY" THEME	unlisted
"THE PERRY COMO SHOW" THEME	unlisted
"PERRY MASON" THEME	unlisted
THE PERSIAN PEARL	I. Fields
	M. Carre
PETE'S FIFTH	C. Brandt
PETER AND THE WOLF	L. Brown
	J. Hill

Composer	Source
A. Glazounov	Raymonda
M. Glinka	Ruslan and Ludmilla
P. Tchaikovsky	Romeo and Juliet (Overture)
F. Mendelssohn	Piano Piece in E flat (Op. 85, #3)
L. Beethoven	Für Elise
L. Beethoven	Symphony 6
L. Beethoven	Sonata for Piano 8 in c (Op. 13)
P. Tchaikovsky	Symphony 6
H. Martin	Breezy and Easy
M. DeLugg	Whenever I'm with You
P. Tchaikovsky	Nutcracker Suite (March)
R. Simon	El Maninsero
J. S. Bach	Cantata 212
S. Prokofiev	Peter and the Wolf
B. Godard	Au Matin
C. Stigman	Dream Along with Me
F. Steiner	Perry Mason Theme
G. Bizet	The Pearl Fishers
P. Tchaikovsky	Symphony 5
S. Prokofiev	Peter and the Wolf

Title	Adapter/Lyricist
"PHILIP MORRIS" THEME	unlisted
PHOEBUS AND PAN	unlisted
A PHOTOGRAPH OF YOU	W. Milton H. Roy
PICK YOURSELF UP	J. Kern
PICKIN' MELODY IN F	F. Morgan S. Jones N. Malkin
THE PICTURE OF FIDELITY	M. Pahl L. Stein C. Warnick G. Leigh V. Leon
THE PIED PIPER	ballet
THE PILGRIMS	unlisted
PILLAR OF FIRE	ballet
PINGPONG FOR BACH BUGS	F. Loffler
PINK CHIFFON	B. Leighton M. Wechsler
PLAY THAT "SONG OF INDIA" AGAIN	unlisted
PLAY THE PLAYERA	X. Cugat E. Drake
A PLEADING	A. Samuelson F. Wishaw
POCO PAVANE	S. Henderson
POEME MYSTIQUE	unlisted

Composer	Source
F. Grofe	Grand Canyon Suite (On the Trail)
J. S. Bach	Cantata 201
F. Mendelssohn	unlisted
B. Smetana	The Merry Chicken Yard
A. Rubenstein	Melody in F
F. Lehar	The Merry Widow
A. Copland	Clarinet Concerto
F. Mendelssohn	Piano Piece in B flat (Op. 67, #3)
A. Schoenberg	Verklärte Nacht
J. S. Bach	Invention 4
G. Verdi	Aida (Celeste Aida)
N. Rimsky-Korsakov	Song of India
E. Granados	Playera
P. Tchaikovsky	unlisted
M. Ravel	Pavan for a Dead Princess
E. Bloch	Sonata for Violin

115

Title	Adapter/Lyricist
"POET'S GOLD" THEME	unlisted
POLISH SYMPHONY	unlisted
POLITICS	E. Harburg
	J. Gorney
"THE POLLY BERGEN SHOW" THEME	unlisted
POLONAISE FOR TWO	J. Latouche
	B. Kaper
POMP AND CIRCUMSTANCE STOMP	W. Herman
	N. Pierce
POPULATION	M. Pahl
	C. Warnick
	E. Eager
	I. Kostal
POSSESSED	A. Ferrante
	L. Teicher
POST HORN SERENADE	unlisted
PRAGUE SYMPHONY	unlisted
PRAYER FOR VICTORY	A. McKee
PRELUDE AND LEGEND	R. Wright
	G. Forrest
PRELUDE TO LOVE	J. Harnell
PRELUDE TO LOVE	J. Harnell
PRESTO PRESTO (SPINNING WHEEL)	R. Lert
	B. Trehaine
	V. Baum
	A. Ronell
PRETENDING	unlisted
PRETTY BUTTERFLY	S. Skylar
"PRETTY KITTY KELLY" THEME	unlisted

Composer	Source
C. Debussy	Clair de Lune
P. Tchaikovsky	Symphony 3
J. Offenbach	La Vie Parisienne
J. Styne	The Party's Over
F. Chopin	Polonaise in A flat
E. Elgar	Pomp and Circumstance
N. Rimsky-Korsakov	unlisted
P. Tchaikovsky	unlisted
W. A. Mozart	Serenade 9 in D (K. 320)
W. A. Mozart	Symphony 38 in D
J. S. Bach	unlisted
E. Grieg	Piano Concerto in a
F. Chopin	Prelude 7
P. Tchaikovsky	unlisted
F. Flotow	unlisted
L. Delibes	Coppelia Waltz
A. Dvorak	Humoresque
J. Molloy	Kerry Dancers

117

Title	Adapter/Lyricist
PRINCE AND PRINCESS	E. Madden
PRINCESS CHA CHA CHA	H. Harden
PRINCESS SCHEHERAZADE	T. Charles
PROVENZA BY THE SEA	M. Valentine
	M. Kay
PUDDLES	C. Warnick
	C. Leigh
THE QUIET HILL	D. Raye
	H. Spina
A QUIET LAND	R. Wright
	G. Forrest
RABBIT DANCE	P. Weston
RACHMANINOFF MEETS PAGANINI	L. Garisto
	J. Wolf
	H. Moss
THE RAGE OVER THE LOST PENNY	unlisted
RAHADLAKUM	G. Forrest
	R. Wright
"THE RAILROAD HOUR" THEME	unlisted
RAIN SONATA	unlisted
RAINBOW IN THE NIGHT	J. Styne
	S. Meyer
RAINBOW THEME	H. Hummell
	H. Whistler
RAINBOW'S END	unlisted

Composer	Source
N. Rimsky-Korsakov	Scheherazade
P. Tchaikovsky	unlisted
N. Rimsky-Korsakov	Scheherazade
G. Verdi	La Traviata
R. Schumann	unlisted
C. Debussy	Beau Soir
S. Rachmaninoff	Symphony 2
S. Prokofiev	Peter and the Wolf
S. Rachmaninoff N. Paganini	Variations on a Theme by Paganini (10th variation) and Paganini, Caprice 24
L. Beethoven	Capriccio in G
A. Borodin	unlisted
traditional	I've Been Working on the Railroad
J. Brahms	Sonata for Violin 1 in G (Op. 78)
P. Tchaikovsky	unlisted
F. Chopin	Fantasie Impromptu
L. Beethoven	Piano Sonata 8 (Pathetique)

119

Title	Adapter/Lyricist
RAINDROP	unlisted
RAKOCZY MARCH	unlisted
RAZOR QUARTET	unlisted
RECOLLECTIONS OF TCHAIKOVSKY	unlisted
"THE RED SKELTON SHOW" THEME	unlisted
REFORMATION SYMPHONY	unlisted
REGRETS	unlisted
LA REINE	unlisted
REMEMBER	D. Bennett
REQUIEM SYMPHONY	unlisted
THE REST OF MY DAYS	L. Pober
RESTLESSNESS	unlisted
RESURRECTION SYMPHONY	unlisted
RETROSPECTION	unlisted
THE RETURN	unlisted
REVERIE	unlisted
REVOLUTIONARY ETUDE	unlisted
RHENISH SYMPHONY	unlisted
RHYMES HAVE I	R. Wright
G. Forrest

Composer	Source
F. Chopin	Prelude 15 in D flat
F. Liszt	Hungarian Dance 15 in a
J. Haydn	String Quartet in f (Op. 55, #2)
P. Tchaikovsky	Piano Concerto 1, Andante Cantabile, 1812 Overture, Symphony 6
D. Rose	Holiday for Strings
F. Mendelssohn	Symphony 5 in d
F. Mendelssohn	Piano Piece in a (Op. 19, #2)
J. Haydn	Symphony 85 in B flat
F. Chopin	unlisted
H. Hanson	Symphony 4
N. Rimsky-Korsakov	Scheherazade
F. Mendelssohn	Piano Piece in f Sharp (Op. 19, #5)
G. Mahler	Symphony 2
F. Mendelssohn	Piano Piece in D (Op. 102, #3)
F. Mendelssohn	Piano Piece in A (Op. 85, #5)
F. Mendelssohn	Piano Piece in F (Op. 85, #1)
F. Chopin	Etude 12 in c (Op. 10)
R. Schumann	Symphony 3
A. Borodin	Prince Igor

Title	Adapter/Lyricist
THE RIDER	unlisted
RIDING HOME	F. Hunter
	H. Scott
RIGOLETTO RAG	R. Linda
RIGOLETTO ROCK	unlisted
RIKARD'S FAREWELL	G. Forrest
	R. Wright
"ROAD OF LIFE" THEME	unlisted
"ROAD OF LIFE" THEME	unlisted
THE ROAD TO ROMANCE	D. Wilson
	E. Bradley
ROCKIN' DON	G. Kingsley
ROCKIN' WITH ROCKY	K. Brown
	J. Hill
THE ROCKIN'S BEE	A. Cain
	L. Merian
ROLLIN' HOME	T. Dorsey
	C. Mastren
ROMANCE	B. Leighton
	M. Wechsler
"ROMANCE OF HELEN TRENT" THEME	unlisted
ROMEO AND JULIET	R. Carter
ROSALINDA	P. Kerby
"ROSEMARY CLOONEY SHOW" THEME	unlisted
RUBENSTEIN'S REFRAIN	B. Ballard
RUSSIAN RAG	unlisted
RUSSIANESQUE	L. Katzman
RUSTIC WEDDING	unlisted

Composer	Source
J. Haydn	String Quartet in g (Op. 74, #3)
A. Dvorak	Symphony 9 (New World)
G. Verdi	Ridoletto
G. Verdi	Rigoletto (Caro Nome)
R. Wright	The Last Spring
P. Tchaikovsky	Andante Cantabile
P. Tchaikovsky	Symphony 6 (1st Movement)
J. Brahms	unlisted
W. Mozart	Don Giovanni (Serenade)
S. Rachmaninoff	Piano Concerto 2
N. Rimsky-Korsakov	Flight of the Bumble Bee
A. Dvorak	Symphony 9 (New World)
V. Bellini	Norma (Casta Diva)
traditional	Juanita
P. Tchaikovsky	Romeo and Juliet (Overture)
J. Strauss	Die Fledermaus
W. Gross	Tenderly
A. Rubenstein	The Old Refrain
S. Rachmaninoff	Prelude in c Sharp
P. Tchaikovsky	unlisted
C. Goldmark	Symphony 1

Title	Adapter/Lyricist
SABER DANCE BOOGIE	L. Busch
"SABER OF LONDON" THEME	unlisted
SAD FAIRY TALE	J. Wolman
SAILIN' ON	G. Kahn
	B. Nathausen
SAILING HOME	T. Powell
	W. Samuels
	L. Whitcup
SAILOR'S FAREWELL	unlisted
ST. ANNE'S FUGUE	unlisted
ST. FRANCIS	ballet
SAMBA PAPAGENO	G. Kingsley
SANDS OF TIME	R. Wright
	G. Forrest
SARAH JACKMAN	A. Sherman
SATURDAY GIRL	E. Maschwitz
	B. Grun
THE SAUCY MAID	unlisted
SAVE ME A DREAM	M. Berle
	N. Kenny
	A. Silver
SAY NO MORE, IT'S GOODBYE	D. Langdon
SAY SI SI	F. Luban
	A. Stillman
	L. Gilbert
SCHEHERAZADE BLUE	T. Charles
THE SCHOOLMASTER	unlisted
SCOTCH SONATA	unlisted

Composer	Source
A. Khatchaturian	Gayne (Saber Dance)
M. Lenard	Saber Theme
D. Shostakovich	unlisted
A. Dvorak	Symphony 9 (New World)
A. Dvorak	Symphony 9 (New World)
F. Mendelssohn	unlisted
J. S. Bach	Fugue for Organ in E flat
P. Hindemith	Noblissima Visione
W. Mozart	The Magic Flute
A. Borodin	In the Steppes of Central Asia
traditional	Frére Jacques
A. Dvorak	unlisted
A. Bruckner	Symphony 1 in c
P. Tchaikovsky	Symphony 5
J. Brahms	Symphony 3
E. Lecuona	Para Vigo Me Voy
N. Rimsky-Korsakov	Scheherazade
J. Haydn	Symphony 55 in E flat
F. Mendelssohn	Fantasie in f Sharp (Op. 28)

Title	Adapter/Lyricist
SCOTCH SYMPHONY	ballet
"SEA HUNT" THEME	unlisted
SEA SYMPHONY	unlisted
SELTZER BOY	A. Sherman
SERAPHIC DIALOG	ballet
SERENADE	A. Ross
SERENADE	A. Silvestri
SERENADE IN THE NIGHT	J. Kennedy
"THE SHADOW" THEME	unlisted
SHALL WE SAY FAREWELL TO SPRING	E. Harburg
	L. Halevy
	H. Meilhac
	J. Gorney
	R. deCormier
"SHELL CHATEAU" THEME	H. Warren
SHEPHERD BOY ETUDE	unlisted
SHEPHERD LULLABY	C. Previn
	R. Freed
SHEPHERD'S COMPLAINT	unlisted
SHEPHERD'S SERENADE see LOVESICK SERENADE	
SHERABOP	unlisted
SHERLOCK HOLMES	unlisted

Composer	Source
F. Mendelssohn	Symphony 3
R. Llewellyn	Sea Hunt Theme
R. Vaughan Williams	Symphony 1
A. Robinson	Water Boy
N. dello Joio	Triumph of St. Joan Symphony
F. Schubert	Serenade
E. Toselli	Rimpianto (Serenade)
C. Bixio L. Cherubini	Violino Tzigane
C. Saint-Saens	Omphale's Spinning Wheel
J. Offenbach	Gaité Parisienne (Waltz)
A. Dubin	About a Quarter to Nine
F. Chopin	Etude #1 in A flat (Op. 25)
W. A. Mozart	unlisted
F. Mendelssohn	Piano Piece in b (Op. 67 (Op. 67, #5)
N. Rimsky-Korsakov	Scheherazade (3rd movement)
A. Sullivan	Ruddigore (March of the Ancestors)

Title	Adapter/Lyricist
"SID CAESAR INVITES YOU" THEME	unlisted
SIGHING WIND	unlisted
SILENT LOVE	C. Deis
	M. Bristol
SILVER BELLS	C. Warnick
	M. Pahl
	E. Eager
SINFONIA ANTARCTICA	unlisted
SING A SMILING SONG	T. Adam
	G. Bruns
SING ME A SONG	E. Maschwitz
	B. Grun
"SINGIN' SAM" THEME	V. Bryan
SIR GREENBAUM'S MADRIGAL	A. Sherman
SIXTY SECOND JUMP	A. Datz
SKIN	A. Sherman
SLAVIC DANCE	B. Hanighen
	L. Jacobson
	S. Stange
	S. Benaver
SMALL TOWN SWEETHEART	E. Maschwitz
	B. Grun
SMILE	G. Parson
	J. Phillips
SNEEZIN' BEE	S. Jones
SO DEEP IS THE NIGHT	A. Stillman

Composer	Source
B. Green	Caesar Theme
F. Mendelssohn	Piano Piece in g (Op. 102, #4)
P. Tchaikovsky	unlisted
N. Rimsky-Korsakov	Christmas Eve Suite
R. Vaughan Williams	Symphony 7
P. Tchaikovsky	unlisted
A. Dvorak	unlisted
G. Edwards	Tammany
King Henry VIII	Greensleeves
F. Chopin	Minute Waltz
R. Adler J. Ross	Heart (Damn Yankees)
O. Straus	unlisted
A. Dvorak	unlisted
C. Chaplin	City Lights (film theme)
N. Rimsky-Korsakov	Flight of the Bumble Bee
F. Chopin	Etude in E

Title	Adapter/Lyricist
SO HELP ME	M. Berle
SO LONG, IT'S BEEN GOOD TO KNOW YOU	W. Guthrie
SO PROUD	R. Wright
	G. Forrest
SODOM AND GOMORRAH	P. Webster
SOFTLY MY LOVE	S. Tepper
	R. Bennett
SOME SONG TCHAIKOVSKY WROTE	unlisted
SOMEHOW WE'VE MADE THE MORNING	unlisted
SOMEHOW YOU KNOW	H. August
	A. Beach
SOMETHING SO DELIGHTFUL	M. Pahl
	C. Warnick
	V. Leon
	C. Leigh
	L. Stein
SOMEWHERE	unlisted
THE SONG FROM "MOULIN ROUGE" see WHERE IS YOUR HEART	
SONG OF DECEMBER	F. Moritt
SONG OF LOVE	A. Ross
SONG OF THE NIGHT	unlisted
SONG OF THE STEPPES	F. Bornschein
SONG OF THE TRAVELER	unlisted
A SONG TO REMEMBER	M. Stoloff
	S. Chaplin
	S. Cahn

Composer	Source
P. Tchaikovsky	Capriccio Italien
traditional	Billy the Kid
S. Rachmaninoff	Symphony 1; Piano Concerto 3
E. di Capua	O Sole Mio
F. Chopin	Etude 1
P. Tchaikovsky	Piano Concerto in b flat
L. Beethoven	Symphony 9 (Ode to Joy)
A. Khachaturian	unlisted
F. Lehar	The Merry Widow
W. Mozart	Piano Sonata in C
F. Mendelssohn	unlisted
F. Schubert	Symphony 8
G. Mahler	Symphony 7
P. Tchaikovsky	Marche Slave
F. Mendelssohn	Piano Piece in B flat (Op. 85, #6)
F. Chopin	Etude in E

Title	Adapter/Lyricist
SONGS MY MOTHER TAUGHT ME	various
THE SORROWFUL SOUL	unlisted
SORRY, MR. BRUBECK, IT'S BACH	F. Loffler
SOTTO VOCE	B. Leighton
	M. Wechsler
SOUVENIR OF FLORENCE	unlisted
SPANISH SERENADE	C. Dragon
	E. Lawrence
	R. Lee
SPECTRE OF THE ROSE	ballet
SPINNING SONG	unlisted
SPRING IN MY HEART	H. Salter
	R. Freed
SPRING LOVE	F. Hunter
	H. Scott
SPRING MAGIC	A. Wilder
	W. Engvick
	H. Reisenfeld
SPRING SONG	unlisted
SPRING SYMPHONY	unlisted
STAND UP AND FIGHT	O. Hammerstein II
STAR AND SHADOWS	N. Luboff
	M. Keith
	A. Bergman
STAR OF EVENING	M. Gold

Composer	Source
A. Dvorak	Melody
F. Mendelssohn	Piano Piece in F (Op. 53, #4)
J. S. Bach	Well-Tempered Clavier 2 (Fugue 1)
G. Verdi	Il Trovatore
P. Tchaikovsky	Sextet in d (Op. 70)
G. Bizet	Carmen
C. Weber	Invitation to the Dance
F. Mendelssohn	Piano Piece in C (Op. 67, #4)
J. Strauss	unlisted
E. Grieg	Piano Concerto in a (second movement)
A. Borodin	String Quartet 2 in D
F. Mendelssohn	Piano Piece in A (Op. 62, #6)
R. Schumann	Symphony 1 in B flat
G. Bizet	Carmen (Toreador Song)
C. Debussy	Beau Soir
R. Wagner	Tannhaüser (Evening Star)

Title	Adapter/Lyricist
STAR OF LOVE	J. Oliver
	A. Mattullath
STARRY NIGHT OF SPLENDOR	E. Lorenz
	R. Yale
STARS NEVER CRY	M. Berle
	B. Kroll
STARLIGHT ARIA	R. Lewis
"STELLA DALLAS" THEME	unlisted
"THE STEVE ALLEN SHOW" THEME	unlisted
THE STILL POINT	ballet
STOLEN KISSES	F. Steininger
STORM QUINTET	unlisted
THE STORY OF A STARRY NIGHT	A. Hoffman
	M. Kurtz
	J. Livingston
"STORY OF MARY MARLIN" see "MARY MARLIN"	
STRANGE MUSIC	R. Wright
	G. Forrest
STRANGER IN PARADISE	R. Wright
	G. Forrest
THE STREETS OF MIAMI	A. Sherman
	L. Busch
STRINGING ALONG WITH FAUST	J. Gleason
	J. Barbier
	M. Carre
STRINGS AT THE HOP	unlisted

Composer	Source
I. Albeniz	unlisted
F. Mendelssohn	A Midsummer Night's Dream (Nocturne)
F. Schubert	Serenade
G. Puccini	Tosca
traditional	How Can I Leave Thee?
S. Allen	You're the One for Me (opening) and Impossible (closing)
C. Debussy	String Quartet in g
P. Tchaikovsky	Swan Lake and Quartet in D
L. Beethoven	Quintet for Strings in C (Op. 29)
P. Tchaikovsky	Symphony 6 in b
E. Grieg	Peer Gynt (Wedding Day at Troldhaugen)
A. Borodin	Polovtsian Dances
traditional	The Streets of Laredo
C. Gounod	Faust
P. Tchaikovsky	Symphony 6

135

Title	Adapter/Lyricist
STROLLIN' HOME	B. Bain
	J. Krause
	B. Willie
STROLLING PROMENADE	B. Leighton
	M. Wechsler
"STUDIO ONE" THEME	unlisted
SUDDENLY	D. Cochran
SUGAR PLUM CHA CHA	H. Harden
SUGAR RUM CHERRY	D. Ellington
	B. Strayhorn
SUMMER MOON	L. Sugar
	J. Klenner
SUMMER SONG	E. Maschwitz
	B. Grun
THE SUNRISE	unlisted
SUNRISE IN PARIS	M. Pahl
	C. Warnick
	I. Kostal
SUNRISE SYMPHONY	unlisted
SUSPENDED AUTOMATION	B. Leighton
	M. Wechsler
SWAN SONG	unlisted
SWAN SONG	R. Maltby
SWAN SPLASHDOWN	unlisted
THE SWAN SWINGS	L. Brown
	J. Hill
THE SWAN'S SONG	C. Solzido
	S. Yarrow

Composer	Source
A. Dvorak	Symphony 9 (New World)
G. Puccini	Gianni Schicchi
B. Herrmann	Studio One Theme
R. Heuburger	The Opera Ball
P. Tchaikovsky	The Nutcracker Suite
P. Tchaikovsky	The Nutcracker Suite
I. Stravinsky	Firebird Suite
A. Dvorak	unlisted
J. Haydn	String Quartet in B flat (Op. 76, #4)
J. Strauss	unlisted
J. Haydn	Symphony 94 in G
G. Rossini	Barber of Seville (Una Voce Poco Fa)
J. Haydn	String Quartet in B flat (Op. 103)
P. Tchaikovsky	Swan Lake
P. Tchaikovsky	Swan Lake
P. Tchaikovsky	Swan Lake
C. Saint-Saens	The Swan

Title	Adapter/Lyricist
SWEET MEMORIES	J. Wisner
SWEET REMEMBRANCE	unlisted
SWING A LA TURCA	G. Kingsley
SWINGIN' AT IGOR'S	unlisted
SWINGIN' BACH GUITAR	F. Loffler
SWINGIN' LITTLE MARTHA	unlisted
SWINGIN' THE BLUE DANUBE	S. Cooley
SWINGIN' THE TOREADOR	B. Kessel
	H. Meilhac
	L. Halevy
THE SWINGING PLUM FAIRY	M. Rogers
TAKE ME TONIGHT	W. Gold
	R. Schroeder
	R. Alfred
TALE OF PETER AND THE WOLF	H. Rome
"A TALE OF TODAY" THEME	unlisted
TAMBARINA	D. Coleman
TARA TALARRA TALAR	J. Farrow
	M. Symes
TARANTELLE	unlisted
THE TARTAR SONG	M. Pahl
	C. Warnick
	E. Eager
TCHAIKOVSKY TAG	B. Green
TEARS FALL IN MY HEART	N. Page
	P. Verlaine
	A. Mattullath

Composer	Source
F. Liszt	unlisted
F. Mendelssohn	Piano Piece in E (Op. 19, #1)
W. A. Mozart	Rondo a la Turca
A. Borodin	Prince Igor (Polovtsian Dances)
J. S. Bach	Invention 8
F. von Flotow	Martha (M'apari)
J. Strauss	Blue Danube Waltz
G. Bizet	Carmen
P. Tchaikovsky	Nutcracker Suite
P. Tchaikovsky	Symphony 6 (1st movement)
S. Prokofiev	Peter and the Wolf
G. Meyerbeer	Le Prophete (Coronation March)
V. Monte	Czardas
traditional	Vieni sul Mar
F. Mendelssohn	Piano Piece in C (Op. 102, #3)
N. Rimsky-Korsakov	unlisted
P. Tchaikovsky	unlisted
C. Debussy	Ariettes Oubliees

139

Title	Adapter/Lyricist
TECLA'S MOOD	unlisted
TED MALONE see "BETWEEN THE BOOKENDS"	
"THE TELEPHONE HOUR" THEME	unlisted
TELL ME DAISY	H. Berte S. Romberg H. Reichert D. Donnelly
TELL ME WE'LL MEET AGAIN	I. Kallman M. Carson
THE TEMPEST	unlisted
THAT PRELUDE!	R. Wright G. Forrest
THAT'LL BE THE DAY	E. Harburg H. Kay
THAT'S WHAT VIENNA'S FOR	M. Pahl C. Warnick I. Kostal
THAT'S WHERE YOU ARE	P. Springer S. Gallop
THEME AND VARIATIONS	ballet
THEN I WROTE THE MINUET IN G	F. Loesser M. Malneck
THERE ONCE WAS AN INDIAN MAID	traditional
THERE'S NO TOMORROW	A. Hoffman L. Corday L. Carr
THEY CAN'T CATCH ME	P. Weston O. Nash
THESE ARE THE THINGS I LOVE	H. Barlow

Composer	Source
F. Chopin	Scherzo 2 in b flat
D. Voorhees	The Bell Waltz
F. Schubert	unlisted
G. Verdi	unlisted
L. Beethoven	Sonata for Piano 17 in d (Op. 31)
S. Rachmaninoff	Prelude in c Sharp 2 (Op. 3)
J. Offenbach	unlisted
J. Strauss	unlisted
P. Tchaikovsky	unlisted
P. Tchaikovsky	Suite 3
L. Beethoven	Minuet in G
R. Schumann	The Happy Farmer
E. di Capua	O Sole Mio
S. Prokofiev	Peter and the Wolf
P. Tchaikovsky	Romance

Title	Adapter/Lyricist
THE THING	C. Green
THIS FAIR AND BEAUTEOUS SONG	S. Gaines
THIS IS MY BELOVED see AND THIS IS MY BELOVED	
THIS IS MY KIND OF LOVE	R. Wright G. Forrest
THOUGH LIGHT IS MY HEART	S. Gaines
A THOUSAND AND ONE NIGHTS	T. Mossman J. Segal
THREE LOVES	R. Wright G. Forrest
THREE ORANGES	L. Brown
THREE VIRGINS AND A DEVIL	ballet
THREE'S A CROWD	F. Steininger F. Brown
THROUGH THE SILENT NIGHT	V. Harris C. Manney
THROUGH THE YEARS	C. DeBrant J. Fey
THE THUNDERSTORM	unlisted
THWARTED THWARTED, CURSES CURSES	L. Halevy H. Meilhac E. Eager
TILL THE END OF TIME	T. Mossman
A TIME, A PLACE, A GIRL	J. Harnell
TINGA LINGA LINGA	E. Maxwell S. Miller L. Orenstein

Composer	Source
traditional	Chandler's Wife
F. Chopin	unlisted
S. Rachmaninoff	Piano Concerto 2
D. Scarlatti	Serenata
N. Rimsky-Korsakov	Scheherazade
E. Grieg	Poem Erotique (Erotik) & Albumblatt
S. Prokofiev	Love for Three Oranges (March)
O. Respighi	Ancient Airs and Dances
P. Tchaikovsky	unlisted
S. Rachmaninoff	Romance 3
J. Sibelius	Finlandia
W. A. Mozart	Contradanse for Orchestra (K. 534)
J. Offenbach	Tales of Hoffman
F. Chopin	Polonaise in A flat
N. Rimsky-Korsakov	Scheherazade
F. Chopin	unlisted

Title	Adapter/Lyricist
TIT WILLOW TWIST	M. Browning
THE TITAN	unlisted
TO ELISE WITH LOVE	G. Sonneborn
TO HORA'S AID	N. Hefti
TO LOVE A DREAM	T. Mossman
TO LOVE AGAIN	E. Duchin
TO ME YOU'RE A SONG	B. Merrill
TO MY BELOVED	F. Feibel
"TODAY'S CHILDREN" THEME	unlisted
"TOM MIX" THEME	unlisted
"TOMBSTONE TERRITORY" THEME	unlisted
TONIGHT WE LOVE	B. Wirth
TONIGHT YOU'RE MINE	unlisted
"TONY WONS' SCRAPBOOK" THEME	unlisted
"TONY WONS' SCRAPBOOK" THEME	unlisted
TOOT TOOT TOOTIE TOOT	D. Ellington
	B. Strayhorn
THE TOP	E. Haensch
TOP OF THE MOON	I. Cook
	R. Gilbert
	H. Kalin
	L. Rellstab
THE TOREADOR FIGHTS THE RABBIT	A. Musolino

Composer	Source
A. Sullivan	The Mikado
G. Mahler	Symphony 1 in D
L. Beethoven	Für Elise
N. Rimsky-Korsakov	Scheherazade
N. Rimsky-Korsakov	Coq d'Or (Hymn to the Sun)
F. Chopin	Nocturne in E flat
F. Chopin	Chopin Etude 3
J. Massenet	Elegie
unlisted	Aphrodite
unlisted	When It's Roundup Time in Texas
W. Backer	Tombstone Territory Theme
P. Tchaikovsky	Piano Concerto 1
P. Tchaikovsky	Piano Concerto 1
E. Elgar	Salut d'Amour
R. Schumann	Traumerei
P. Tchaikovsky	The Nutcracker Suite
G. Bizet	Petite Suite
F. Schubert	Serenade
G. Bizet	Carmen

Title	Adapter/Lyricist
EL TORITO (THE LITTLE BULL)	W. Foster
	T. Pierce
	H. Meilhac
	L. Halevy
TORRENT	unlisted
TOWARD THE END OF THE DAY	A. Stillman
	M. Jeffreys
"TOWN HALL TONIGHT" see "THE FRED ALLEN SHOW"	
TOY SYMPHONY	unlisted
TRAGIC OVERTURE	unlisted
TRAVEL AGENCY	M. Pahl
	C. Warnick
	I. Kostal
"TREASURE HUNT" THEME	unlisted
TREES	O. Rasbach
TRIANGLE CONCERTO	unlisted
TROUT QUINTET	unlisted
TRUMPET PLAYER'S LULLABY	G. Sonneborn
"TRUTH OR CONSEQUENCES" THEME	unlisted
TURKISH CONCERTO	unlisted
TURKISH MOON	J. Messner
TWANGY SERENADE	unlisted
TWELFTH STREET TOREADOR	V. Alexander
	H. Meilhac
	L. Halevy
"THE TWENTIETH CENTURY" THEME	unlisted

Composer	Source
G. Bizet	Carmen
F. Chopin	Etude 4 in c Sharp (Op. 10)
L. Delibes	unlisted
J. Haydn	Symphony in C
J. Brahms	Overture in d (Op. 81)
J. Strauss	unlisted
M. DeLugg	Treasure Hunt Theme
N. Rimsky-Korsakov	The Hindu Song
F. Liszt	Concerto for Piano 1 in E flat
F. Schubert	Quintet in A (Op. 114)
J. Brahms	Cradle Song
traditional	Merrily We Roll Along
W. A. Mozart	Concerto for Violin 5 in A (K. 219)
W. A. Mozart	Rondo a la Turca
F. Schubert	Serenade
G. Bizet	Carmen
G. Anthiel	Main Title Theme

Title	Adapter/Lyricist
TWILIGHT	A. Goodman
	G. Shelley
	L. Rubenstein
TWILIGHT	A. Goodman
	G. Shelley
	L. Rubenstein
TWO SILHOUETTES IN THE MOONLIGHT	M. Sanders
TZENA, TZENA, TZENA	I. Myers
	Y. Haggiz
	M. Parish
UNDER THE LILAC BOUGH	A. Ross
	H. Clutsam
	A. Wilner
UNDERNEATH MY LADY'S WINDOW	M. Liebman
	C. Warnick
UNEASY LIES THE HEAD	E. Eager
"THE U. S. STEEL HOUR" THEME	unlisted
UNTO THEE I LIFT MINE EYES	J. Wilson
VALE OF SHADOW	C. Botsford
"VALIANT LADY" THEME	unlisted
LA VALSE	ballet
VENETIAN LOVE SONG	I. Fields
	M. Carre
	C. Corman
VERY BRITISH, MR. BACH	F. Loffler
"VIC AND SADE" THEME	unlisted
VICTORY SYMPHONY	unlisted

Composer	Source
A. Borodin	Prince Igor (Polovtsian Dances)
A. Borodin	unlisted
Z. Fibich	Poème
traditional	Hebrew folk tune
F. Schubert	Lilac Time
J. Strauss	unlisted
N. Rimsky-Korsakov	unlisted
B. Green	U. S. Steel Theme
L. Beethoven	Sonata for Piano 14
J. Sibelius	traditional
M. Ponce	Estrellita
M. Ravel	La Valse and Valses Nobles et Sentimentales
G. Bizet	unlisted
J. S. Bach	English Suite 3 (Gavotte)
J. Balough	Chanson Bohemienne
L. Beethoven	Symphony 5

149

Title	Adapter/Lyricist
VIENNA WOODS CHA CHA CHA	I. Fields
VILLAGE HOP HOP	B. Grun
VIVE LA VIRTUE	E. Harburg
THE VODKA BOAT SONG	L. Brown
	J. Hill
VODKA! VODKA!	R. Wright
	G. Forrest
"THE VOICE OF FIRESTONE" THEME	unlisted
VOLGA VOUTY	D. Ellington
	B. Strayhorn
WAIT TILL THE CLOUDS ROLL BY	unlisted
WAKE WITH THE DAWN	L. Finley
WALDSTEIN SONATA	unlisted
WALK WITH ME	G. Cates
	L. Gordon
	I. Taylor
WALTZ SERENADE	E. Brent
THE WANDERER	unlisted
WANDERER FANTASY	unlisted
WARM KISSES IN THE COOL OF THE NIGHT	B. Kaye
WAS I WAZIR?	R. Wright
	G. Forrest
WATER MUSIC	P. Weston
	O. Nash

Composer	Source
J. Strauss	Tales from the Vienna Woods
B. Smetana	unlisted
J. Offenbach	La Belle Hélène
traditional (Russia)	Song of the Volga Boatman
S. Rachmaninoff	Polka Italienne
I. Firestone	If I Could Tell You
P. Tchaikovsky	The Nutcracker Suite (Russian Dance)
J. Haydn	String Quartet in F (Op. 77, #2)
R. Leoncavallo	Mattinata
L. Beethoven	Sonata for Piano 21 in C (Op. 53)
A. Dvorak	unlisted
P. Tchaikovsky	Serenade for Strings
F. Mendelssohn	Piano Piece in b (Op. 30, #4)
F. Schubert	Fantasy 15 in C (Op. 15)
P. Tchaikovsky	Swan Lake
A. Borodin	String Quartet 2 in D
S. Prokofiev	Peter and the Wolf

Title	Adapter/Lyricist
"WE ARE FOUR" THEME	L. Pollack
WE GO OUR WAY	M. Pahl
	C. Warnick
	I. Kostal
"WE THE PEOPLE" THEME	unlisted
WE WOULD BE BUILDING	L. Curry
WEDDING BOUQUET	A. Keefer
WEDDING CAKE	unlisted
WEDDING CANTATAS	unlisted
WELCOME SWEET SPRINGTIME	H. Frey
	P. Sykema
"WELLS FARGO" THEME	M. Greene
"WEST POINT" THEME	unlisted
WHAT CHILD IS THIS?	various
WHAT FOR?	J. Klenner
WHATEVER THAT MAY BE	E. Harburg
"WHAT'S MY LINE?" THEME	unlisted
"WHEN A GIRL MARRIES" THEME	unlisted
WHEN I WRITE MY SONG	T. Mossman
WHEN I'M WITH YOU	H. Potter
	E. Dorr
	J. Jewels
WHEN THE LEMON TREES BLOSSOM	A. Winter

Composer	Source
E. Rapee	Diane
J. Strauss	unlisted
J. Brahms	Symphony 1 (last movement)
J. Sibelius	Finlandia
R. Wagner	Lohengrin (Wedding March)
C. Saint-Saens	Valse Caprice (Op. 76)
J. S. Bach	Cantatas 195, 196, 202, 210
A. Rubenstein	Melody in F
S. Wilson	Wells Fargo Theme
P. Egner A. Parham	West Point March
King Henry VIII	Greensleeves
F. Chopin	Prelude 15 (Op. 28)
J. Offenbach	La Belle Hélène
M. DeLugg L. Busch	Roller Coaster
R. Drigo	Serenade
C. Saint-Saens	Samson and Delilah (My Heart at Thy Sweet Voice)
E. Grieg	unlisted
J. Strauss	unlisted

Title	Adapter/Lyricist
WHEN THE LILAC BLOOM INCLOSES	A. Ross
WHEN THERE'S NO YOU	M. Reed
	D. Rae
WHERE ART THOU?	S. Henderson
WHERE DID YOU GET THAT HAT?	J. Sullivan
WHERE IS YOUR HEART?	W. Engvick
WHILE THERE'S A SONG TO SING	F. Steininger
	F. Brown
WHISPER A WORD OF LOVE	H. Rome
WHISPERING WINDS	I. Cheyette
	C. Roberts
A WHITE SHADE OF PALE	Procol Harum
WHIZZING AWAY ALONG DE TRACK	R. Bennett
	O. Hammerstein
	H. Meilhac
	L. Halevy
WHO KNOWS?	G. Lessner
	R. Sour
WHO, ME?	M. Pahl
	C. Warnick
	E. Eager
WHOSE DREAM ARE YOU	M. Willson
WHY	B. Douglas
	B. Martini
WHY SHOULD WE DENY OUR LOVE	J. Barbier
	M. Pahl
	C. Warnick
WIEN SWINGS	J. Herron
	C. Haffner
	R. Genee

Composer	Source
F. Schubert	Lilac Time
R. Leoncavallo	Pagliacci (Vesti la Giuba)
P. Tchaikovsky	unlisted
R. Wagner	Lohengrin
G. Auric	Moulin Rouge (film theme)
P. Tchaikovsky	unlisted
J. Massenet	Meditation
F. Mendelssohn	unlisted
J. S. Bach	Sleeper's Awake
G. Bizet	Carmen
J. Strauss	unlisted
N. Rimsky-Korsakov	unlisted
M. McIntyre	Suite
R. Drigo	Les Millions d'Arlequin (Serenade)
J. Offenbach	Tales of Hoffman
J. Strauss	Alt Wein

Title	Adapter/Lyricist
WILD HORSES	N. Rimsky-Korsak(
WILLIAM TELL RAG	S. Jones
	F. Morgan
WILLIAM TELL RIDES AGAIN	R. Hermann
WINTER DREAMS	unlisted
WINTER LAMENT	B. Thebom
WINTER NIGHT	J. Klenner
THE WINTER WIND	unlisted
WISHING WELL	B. Bonacio
	H. Jerome
	M. King
WITCHES' MINUET	unlisted
WITHOUT REPOSE	unlisted
WON'T YOU COME HOME, DISRAELI	A. Sherman
	L. Busch
WORK SONG	I. Taylor
	H. Stanley
WORLD OUTSIDE	C. Sigman
WORLDS	M. Pahl
	C. Warnick
	E. Eager
WRONG MAN BLUES	E. Brandt
	S. Meyer
	H. Meilhac
XANADU	M. Pahl
	C. Warnick
	E. Eager
	C. Huxley

Composer	Source
R. Schumann	Wild Horseman
G. Rossini	William Tell (Overture)
G. Rossini	William Tell (Overture)
P. Tchaikovsky	Symphony 1
F. Chopin	unlisted
F. Chopin	Prelude 4 (Op. 28)
F. Chopin	Etude 11 in a (Op. 25)
L. Beethoven	Für Elise
J. Haydn	String Quartet in d (Op. 76, #2)
F. Mendelssohn	Piano Piece in b flat (Op. 30, #2)
H. Cannon	Bill Bailey
E. Grieg	Peer Gynt (Wedding Day at Troldhaugen)
R. Addinsell	Warsaw Concerto
N. Rimsky-Korsakov	unlisted
G. Bizet	Carmen (Habañera)
N. Rimsky-Korsakov	Capriccio Espagnole

Title	Adapter/Lyricist
YEARS AND YEARS AGO	D. Bergman
	J. Segal
YES, MY DARLING DAUGHTER	J. Lawrence
YES OR NO	E. Kunneke
	H. Smith
YODEL DE HI	C. Warnick
	C. Leigh
YOU	M. Frank
	S. Skylar
YOU ARE LIKE A FLOWER	N. Luboff
	R. Lee
	C. Dragon
YOU ARE MY DREAM	O. Tucker
YOU ARE MY SUNLIGHT	unlisted
YOU ARE THERE	unlisted
YOU ARE REMEMBERED	unlisted
"YOU BET YOUR LIFE" THEME	H. Ruby
YOU NEED AN ANALYST	A. Sherman
	L. Busch
YOU, ONLY YOU	J. Klenner
YOU TALK JUST LIKE MY MAW	R. Bennett
	O. Hammerstein II
	E. Meilhac
	L. Halevy
YOU TAUGHT ME LOVE	C. Brecken
	B. Harris
	B. Harrington
YOU WENT THE WRONG WAY, OLD KING LOUIE	A. Sherman

158

Composer	Source
E. Toselli	Rimpianto (Serenade)
traditional	Oi Neh Chodeh Hretchew
J. Offenbach	unlisted
R. Schumann	unlisted
G. Puccini	La Bohéme (Musetta's Waltz Song)
R. Schumann	unlisted
A. Rubenstein	unlisted
E. di Capua	O Sole Mio
J. Brahms	Symphony 3
P. Tchaikovsky	Symphony 6
B. Kalman	Hooray for Captain Spaulding
A. Sullivan	The Mikado (I've Got a Little List)
F. Chopin	Ballade 1 (Op. 23)
G. Bizet	Carmen
P. Mascagni	unlisted
J. Brooks	You've Come a Long
S. Russell	Way from St. Louis

159

Title	Adapter/Lyricist
YOU'LL BE SEEING ME	M. Pahl
	C. Warnick
	E. Eager
	I. Kostal
YOU'LL LOVE LOVE IN PAREE	M. Pahl
	C. Warnick
	L. Stein
	V. Leon
	C. Leigh
YOU'LL LOVE ME YET	R. Lewis
"YOUNG WIDDER BROWN" THEME	unlisted
YOUR KISS	M. Greenfield
YOU'RE BREAKING MY HEART	P. Genaro
	S. Skylar
YOU'RE MY TREASURE	unlisted
YOURS	J. Sherr
YOUR KISS	N. Luboff
	M. Keith
	A. Bergman

Composer	Source
N. Rimsky-Korsakov	unlisted
F. Lehar	The Merry Widow
J. Brahms	Symphony 3
A. Harrison M. Arred	In the Gloaming
J. Caretta	unlisted
R. Leoncavallo	Mattinata
E. Becucci	Tesoro Mio
G. Roig	Quiérme Mucho
J. Brahms	Symphony 1

COMPOSER INDEX

Composer & Source	Title
ADDINSELL, R. Warsaw Concerto	World Outside
ADLER, R. Damn Yankees	Skin
ALBENIZ, I. Spanish Suite	Granada
ALBENIZ, I. Tango in D	Moonlight Masquerade
ALFVEN H. Swedish Polka	Baby Gotta Have a Little Fun
ALL THROUGH THE NIGHT Traditional (Welsh air)	Gently, Lord, O Gently, Lead Us
ALLEN, S. Impossible	The Steve Allen Show

Composer & Source	Title
ALLOUETTE Traditional (France)	Al 'N Yetta
ALTER, L. Manhattan Serenade	"The Easy Aces"
ALTER, L. Rainbow on the River	"Dr. Christian"
ANDERSON, L. Plink, Plank, Plunk	"I've Got a Secret"
ANTHIEL, G. Main Title Theme	"The Twentieth Century"
APHRODITE unlisted	"The Guiding Light" "Today's Children"
APRES DE MA BLONDE Traditional (France)	I Want to Be Near You
THE ARKANSAS TRAVELER Traditional	"The Bob Burns Show"
ARLEN, H. One for My Baby	"Adventures of McGraw"
ARNOLD, M. The Key	The Key to Your Heart
THE ASH GROVE Traditional (Welsh)	Let all Things Now Living
AULD LANGE SYNE Traditional	"Between the Bookends"

Composer & Source	Title
AURIC, G. Moulin Rouge	Where Is Your Heart
BACH, C. P. E. Sonata for Flute in G	Hamburger Sonata
BACH, J. C. Concerto for Harp in D	God Save the Queen (King)
BACH, J. S. Air and 30 Variations	Goldberg Variations
BACH, J. S. Cantata 28	All People That On Earth Do Dwell
BACH, J. S. Cantata 195	Wedding Cantata
BACH, J. S. Cantata 196	Wedding Cantata
BACH, J. S. Cantata 201	Phoebus and Pan
BACH, J. S. Cantata 202	Wedding Cantata
BACH, J. S. Cantata 210	Wedding Cantata
BACH, J. S. Cantata 211	Coffee Cantata
BACH, J. S. Cantata 212	Hey Derry Down Derry Peasant Cantata
BACH, J. S. Concerto for Two Violins	Concerto Barocco
BACH, J. S. Concerto in F	Italian Concerto

165

Composer & Source	Title
BACH, J. S. English Suite 3	Very British, Mr. Bach
BACH, J. S. English Suite 5 (Saraband)	Bach Meets the Bulls
BACH, J. S. French Suite #5 (Gavotte)	Bach Goes to Paris
BACH, J. S. Fugue for Organ in D	Fiddle Fugue
BACH, J. S. Fugue for Organ in E Flat	St. Anne's Fugue
BACH, J. S. Fugue for Organ in G	Bach Mambo Little Fugue
BACH, J. S. Gib dich zufrieden und sei Stille	Lullaby of Bachland
BACH, J. S. Invention 8	Swingin' Bach Guitar
BACH, J. S. Invention 13	Bachomania
BACH, J. S. Invention 14	Pingpong for Bach Bugs
BACH, J. S. Partita 4 (Aria)	Bach's Bag
BACH, J. S. St. Matthew Passion	O Lamb of God Most Stainless

Composer & Source	Title
BACH, J. S. Sleepers Awake	Bach to the Blues A White Shade of Pale
BACH, J. S. Suite for Orchestra 3	Air for the G String Bach's Bedroom Brew
BACH, J. S. Toccata and Fugue in D	Dorian
BACH, J. S. Trumpet Suite	O Praise Him
BACH, J. S. Violin Partita 1	Bach's Mashed Bourree

BACH, J. S.
  Well-Tempered Clavier
	I Like Bach
	Sorry, Mr. Brubeck,
	  It's Bach

BACKER, W. Tombstone Territory Theme	"Tombstone Territory"

BALL, E.
  When Irish Eyes Are
    Smiling
	"Duffy's Tavern "

BALOUGH, J. Chanson Bohemienne	"Vic and Sade "
BARGONI, C. Autumn Concerto	And That Reminds Me
BARNES, S. Destiny Waltz	"One Man's Family"

BECKET, T.
  Britannia, The Pride of
    the Ocean
	Columbia, the Gem of
	    the Ocean
	"Don Winslow of the
	    Navy"

167

Composer & Source	Title
BECUCCI, E. Tesoro Mio	You're My Treasure
BEETHOVEN, L. Capriccio in G	The Rage Over the Lost Penny
BEETHOVEN, L. Concerto for Piano 5 in E Flat	Emperor Concerto
BEETHOVEN, L. Für Elise	Elise Passion Flower To Elise with Love Wishing Well
BEETHOVEN, L. Minuet in G	Then I Wrote the Minuet in G
BEETHOVEN, L. Piano Piece in B Flat	Last Thought
BEETHOVEN, L. Quintet for Strings in C (Op. 29)	Storm Quintet
BEETHOVEN, L. Sonata for Piano 8 in C	Rainbow's End Pathetique Sonata
BEETHOVEN, L. Sonata for Piano 14	Evening Song Guarda Che Luna Moonlight Madness Moonlight Sonata My Song for You Unto Thee I Lift Mine Eyes
BEETHOVEN, L. Sonata for Piano 17 in D	The Tempest

Composer & Source	Title

BEETHOVEN, L.
   Sonata for Piano 18
     in E Flat
	The Hunt

BEETHOVEN, L.
   Sonata for Piano 21
     in C
	Waldstein Sonata

BEETHOVEN, L.
   Sonata for Piano 23
     in F
	Appassionata

BEETHOVEN, L.
   Sonata for Violin 9
     in A
	Kreutzer Sonata

BEETHOVEN, L.
   Sonata for Violin 10
     in G
	The Cockcrow

BEETHOVEN, L. Symphony 3	The Error-Attica Eroica Symphony
BEETHOVEN, L. Symphony 5	Beethoven Bounce Beethoven's Fifth Da-Da-Da-Daah Fate Symphony Victory Symphony

BEETHOVEN, L.
   Symphony 6
	The Bogey Bayou
	   Revival
	Pastorale Symphony

BEETHOVEN, L.
   Symphony 9
	Hymn to Joy
	Joyful, Joyful, We
	   Adore Thee
	Somehow We've Made
	   the Morning

Composer & Source	Title
BEETHOVEN, L. Symphony in C	Jena Symphony
BEETHOVEN, L. Trio for Piano and Strings 5 in D	The Ghost Trio
BEETHOVEN, L. Trio for Piano and Strings 7 in B flat	Archduke Trio
BEETHOVEN, L. Wellington's Victory	The Bear Went Over the Mountain He's a Jolly Good Fellow
BELIEVE ME IF ALL THOSE ENDEARING YOUNG CHARMS Traditional	"Aunt Jenny"
BELLINI, V. Norma	Romance
BELLINI, V. I Puritani	Nina's Dance
BERLIOZ, H. Damnation of Faust	Hungarian March
BILLY THE KID Traditional	So Long, It's Been Good to Know You
BIXIO, C. Violino Tzigane	Serenade in the Night
BIZET, G. L'Arlesienne Suite	Bizet Has His Day Mademoiselle la Belle Arlesienne

Composer & Source	Title
BIZET, G.	
Carmen	Barbering Bizet
	Bizzy Bizet
	Carmen
	Carmen Boogie
	Carmen Capers
	Carmen on a Spree
	Carmen's Cha Cha
	Carmen's Tango
	Cashier's Lament
	Charmin' Carmen
	Cotton Pickin' Carmen
	Drive With Care
	Flowersville
	Goin' With Carmen
	Habanera Hoe Down
	Here and Now
	I Lost My Shirt
	If You Dig Me
	Kiss Me Carmen
	Lift 'em Up and Put 'em Down
	Like There's No Place Like
	Madrid, Where is My Love
	My Joe
	Near to the Walls of Sevilla
	Nemrac
	Oh, Theodora
	Pad On the Edge of Town
	Pancho the Panther
	Spanish Serenade
	Swingin' the Toreador

Composer & Source	Title
BIZET, G. Carmen (Cont.)	El Torito Twelfth Street Toreador Whizzing Away Along de Track Wrong Man Blues You Talk Just Like My Man Beat Out Dat Rhythm on a Drum De Cards Don't Lie Dat's Love Dere's a Cafe on de Corner Stand Up and Fight
BIZET, G. The Fair Maid of Perth	Danse Bohemienne
BIZET, G. The Pearl Fishers	The Persian Pearl
BIZET, G. Petite Suite	The Top
BLOCH, E. Schelomo	Hebrew Rhapsody
BLOCH, E. Sonata for Violin	Poeme Mystique
BLOCH, R. Toast of the Town	"The Ed Sullivan Show"
BORODIN, A. In the Steppes of Central Asia	Sands of Time
BORODIN, A. Paraphrases for Four Hands	Chopsticks

Composer & Source	Title
BORODIN, A. Prince Igor	And This Is My Beloved He's In Love Lovers in Paradise Not Since Ninevah Olive Tree Rhymes Have I Stranger in Paradise Swingin' at Igor's Twilight
BORODIN, A. Quartet for Strings #2	Baubles, Bangles and Beads Borodin's Bounce Spring Magic Was I Wazir?
BORODIN, A. Serenade	Night of My Nights
BORODIN, A. Symphony 1	Gesticulate
BORODIN, A. Symphony 2	Fate
BOULANGER, G. Avant de Mourir	My Prayer

BRAHMS, J.
Cradle Song
	Brahms for the Cradle
	  Set
	"Hilltop House" Theme
	Lullaby of Love
	Trumpet Player's
	  Lullaby

BRAHMS, J. Hungarian Dance 4	As Years Go By

Composer & Source	Title
BRAHMS, J. Hungarian Dance 5	Hungarian Goulash #5 Hunt's Goulash
BRAHMS, J. May Valse	Beside a Little Brook
BRAHMS, J. Meine Liebe	My Love is Green
BRAHMS, J. Overture in D (Op. 81)	Tragic Overture
BRAHMS, J. Piano Piece (Op. 86, #2)	In Summer Fields

BRAHMS, J.
Requiem
	How Lovely Are Thou
	  Dwellings
	How Lovely Is Thy
	  Dwelling Place

BRAHMS, J. Sandmannchen	The Little Sandman
BRAHMS, J. Sonata for Violin 1 in G	Rain Sonata
BRAHMS, J. Symphony 1	"We the People" Your Kiss
BRAHMS, J. Symphony 3	Say No More, It's Goodbye You Are There You'll Love Me Yet
BRAHMS, J. Variations on a Theme of Paganini	Paganini Variations

Composer & Source	Title

BRAHMS, J.
    Waltz in A Flat
	Love Will Keep Us
	    Young

BRATTON, J. The Teddy Bear's Parade	"Big Jon and Sparky"
BRITTEN, B. Les Illuminations	Illuminations

BRITTEN, B.
    Young Person's Guide
       to the Orchestra
	Fanfare

BROOKS, J.
    You've Come a Long Way
       from St. Louis
	You Went the Wrong
	    Way, Old King Louis

BRUCKNER, A. Symphony 1	The Saucy Maid

CANNON, H.
    Bill Bailey
	Won't You Come Home,
	    Disraeli

CARSON, P. Patricia	"One Man's Family"
CAVALRY OF THE STEPPES Traditional (Russian)	Meadowland
C'EST SI BON unlisted	I See Bones
CHABRIER, E. Espana	Hot Diggety
CHANDLERS'S WIFE Traditional	The Thing
CHAPLIN, C. City Lights	Smile

Composer & Source	Title
CHAPLIN, C. Limelight (film theme)	Eternally
CHARMINADE, C. Autumn	Autumn Reverie
CHAUSSON, E. Poeme for Violin	Jardin aux Lilas
CHOPIN, F. Ballade 1	You, Only You
CHOPIN, F. Etude	Lover's Concerto
CHOPIN, F. Etude 3 (Op. 10) in E	Flow, River, Flow Just For Tonight No Other Love So Deep is the Night A Song to Remember To Me You're a Song
CHOPIN, F. Etude 4 in C Sharp	Torrent
CHOPIN, F. Etude 5 in G Flat	An Imperial Conference Black Key
CHOPIN, F. Etude 12 in C	Revolutionary Etude
CHOPIN, F. Etude 13 in A Flat (Op. 25)	Aeolian Harp Shepherd Boy Etude Softly My Love
CHOPIN, F. Etude 15 in F	Cartwheel

Composer & Source	Title

CHOPIN, F.
  Etude 23 in G Flat
    (Op. 25)
	Butterfly

CHOPIN, F. Etude 24 in A	Winter Wind

CHOPIN, F.
  Fantasie Impromptu in
    C Sharp
	Choppin' Chopin
	I Wonder As I Wander
	I'm Always Chasing
	  Rainbows
	My Dreams Are Only
	  Driftwood
	Rainbow Theme

CHOPIN, F. The Maiden's Wish	Autumn Song
Chopin, F. Mazurka 5 in B Flat	Au Revoir, Soldier Meadow Lark
CHOPIN, F. Minuets (Op. 70)	Moonlight Minuet
CHOPIN, F. Nocturne 1 (Op. 9)	April in the Rain

CHOPIN, F.
  Nocturne 2 (Op. 9)
    in E Flat
	I Know I Love You
	An Improvisation
	  on Chopin
	My Twilight
	O Heart of My
	  Country
	To Love Again

CHOPIN, F.
  Nocturne 5 in
    F Sharp
	Moonlight Soliloquy

Composer & Source	Title
CHOPIN, F. Polonaise 3	Parading in the Park
CHOPIN, F. Polonaise 6 in A Flat	Cheek to Cheek For the Love of Me Polonaise for Two Till the End of Time
CHOPIN, F. Prelude 4 (Op. 28)	Winter Night
CHOPIN, F. Prelude 7 in A (Op. 28)	Apart I Found You in the Rain The Little Things We Love Prelude to Love
CHOPIN, F. Prelude 15 (Op. 28)	What For? Raindrop
CHOPIN, F. Scherzo 2 in B Flat	Tecla's Mood
CHOPIN, F. Variations on a French Air	Gavotte
CHOPIN, F. Waltz 1 (Op. 64)	No Time Dog Waltz
CHOPIN, F. Waltz 2	The Last Waltz
CHOPIN, F. Waltz 6 in D Flat	Castle of Dreams Mile A Minute Waltz

Composer & Source	Title
CHOPIN, F. Waltz 6 in D Flat	Minutes with Magnante Sixty Second Jump Minute Waltz
CHOPIN, F. Waltz 7 in C Sharp	Choppin' at Chopin
CHOPIN, F. Waltz 9 in A Flat (Op. 69)	Adieu Valse Now I Know Your Face By Heart
CITORELLO, P. Luna Mezzo Mare	Lazy Mary
COATES, E. White Horse Inn	Goodbye
COPLAND, A. Concerto for Clarinet	The Pied Piper
COPLAND, A. Dance Symphony	Grogh
COWARD, N. Someday I'll Find You	"Mr. Keen, Tracer of Lost Persons"
CUI, C. Paraphrases for Four Hands	Chopsticks
DAWES, C. Melody	It's All in the Game
DE CURTIS, E. Torna a Surriento	Only Once
DEBUSSY, C. Afternoon of a Faun	Afternoon Dream
DEBUSSY, C. Ariettes Oubliees	Tears Fall in My Heart

Composer & Source	Title
DEBUSSY, C. Beau Soir	Evening Fair Quiet Hill Star and Shadows
DEBUSSY, C. Clair de Lune	"Mary Marlin" Moonlight Love "The Family Hour" "Moon River" "Poet's Gold"
DEBUSSY C. Nuit d'Etoilles	Dinna Marie
DEBUSSY, C. Quartet for Strings in G	Still Point
DEBUSSY, C. Reverie	Debussy's Dream My Reverie
DE FUENTES, S. Miriame Asi	Grant Those Glances Look At Me
DELIBES, L. Coppelia	Pretending
DELIUS, . Les Filles de Cadiz	Bolero

DELLO JOIO, N.
  Triumph of St. Joan
    Symphony
	Seraphic Dialog

DE LUGG, M. Roller Coaster	"What's My Line?"
DE LUGG, M. Treasure Hunt Theme	"Treasure Hunt"

Composer & Source	Title
DE LUGG, M. Whenever I'm With You	"The Paul Winchell Show"
DENZA, L. Funiculi, Funicula	"Lorenzo Jones"
DIAMOND, D. Rounds for Orchestra	Dance for Walt Whitman
DI CAPUA, E. O Sole Mio	Sodom and Gomorrah There's No Tomorrow You Are My Sunlight
DI CAPUA, E. Oh, Marie	"Life With Luigi"
DODI LI Traditional	Dorie
DRIGO, R. Serenade	"When a Girl Marries" Why
DRIGO, R. Valse Bluette	"Big Sister"
DURAND, P. Bolero	All My Love
DUBIN, A. About a Quarter to Nine	"Shell Chateau"
DVORAK, A. Gypsy Song	Gypsy's Liberty
DVORAK, A. Humoresque	Haunting Humoresque Humorescapade Humoresque Novelty Humorous Humoresque

Composer & Source	Title
DVORAK, A. Humoresque (Cont.)	In Your Moonlit Bower Mammy's Lullaby Pretty Butterfly
DVORAK, A. Melody	Songs My Mother Taught Me
DVORAK, A. Slavonic Dance 4	I'll Be Remembering
DVORAK, A. Symphony 9 (New World)	Cotton Tail Deep Blue Evening From the New World Goin' Home Heart Divine Homesville Massa Dear New World Jump New World Symphony New World's On Its Way New World Rock Riding Home Rollin' Home Sailin' On Sailing Home Strollin' Home
DVORAK, A. Trio in E	Dumky Trio
EDWARDS, G. Sunbonnet Sue	"David Harum"
EDWARDS, G. Tammany	"Singin' Sam"

Composer & Source	Title
EGNER, P. West Point March	"West Point"
ELGAR, E. Cockaigne Overture	In London Town
ELGAR, E. Pomp and Circumstance	Pomp and Circumstance Stomp
ELGAR, E. Salut d'Amour	"Tony Wons' Scrapbook "Betty and Bob"
ELGAR, E. Three Bavarian Dances	The Marksman
ELGAR, E. Variations for Orchestra (Op. 36)	Enigma Variations
FALLA, M. El Amor Brujo	Dance of the Matador
FALVO, R. Dicitencello Vuie	Just Say I Love Her
FIBICH, Z. Cathedral Meditation	Moonlight and Roses
FIBICH, Z. Poème	"Joyce Jordan" Moonlight Madonna Two Silhouettes in the Moonlight
FIRESTONE, I. If I Could Tell You	"The Voice of Firestone"
FLOTOW, F. Martha	The Last Rose of Summer Martha, Martha

Composer & Source	Title

FLOTOW, F.
  Martha (Cont.)
	Martha, Martha Cha
	  Cha, Cha
	Swingin' Little
	  Martha

FOSTER, S. Aura Lee	Love Me Tender
FRANCK, C. Panis Angelicus	Nation's Prayer
FRANCK, C. traditional	The Lord's Prayer
FRERE JACQUES traditional	Sarah Jackman

FRIML, R.
  Smile, Darn Ya, Smile
	"The Fred Allen
	  Show"

FRIML, R. Sympathy	Donkey Serenade
FUENTES, S. DE Miriame Asi	Look At Me
GADE, J. Jalousie	Leprosy

GARLAND, H.
  Sugarfoot Rag
	"Country Music
	  Jubilee"

GLAZOUNOV, A. Raymonda	Pas de Dix
GLINKA, M. Ruslan and Ludmilla	Pas de Trois
GLOVER, C. Rose of Tralee	"Backstage Wife"

Composer & Source	Title

GODARD, B.
  Au Matin
	"Pepper Young's
	  Family"

GODARD, B. Berceuse	Love Sings a Lullaby
GODDARD, P. Melody	In the Moon Mist
GOEDEN, J. Poor Butterfly	"Myrt and Marge"
GOLDMARK, C. Symphony 1	In the Garden Rustic Wedding
GOTTSCHALK, L. The Banjo	Banjo

GOUNOD, C.
  Faust
	Marguerita Waltz
	Stringing Along with
	  Faust

GRANADOS, E. Playera	Play the Players
GRANADOS, E. Spanish Dance	I Can't Remember
GRIEG, E. Albumblatt	Three Loves

GREEN, B.
  Caesar Theme
	"Sid Caesar Invites
	  You"

GREEN, B. U. S. Steel Theme	"The U. S. Steel Hour"
GRIEG, E. Concerto for Piano in A	Grieg's Concerto March Hill of Dreams

Composer & Source	Title

GRIEG, E.
  Concerto for Piano in A
    (Cont.)
	How Can I Tell You
	I Look At Heaven
	Prelude and Legend
	Spring Love

GRIEG, E. Erotik	Eros Three Loves
GRIEG, E. Ich Liebe Dich	I Love You
GRIEG, E. The Last Spring	Rikard's Farewell

GRIEG, E.
  Norwegian Dances
	At the Zoo
	Flim Flam Floo
	Freddy and His Fiddle
	I Can't Dance
	A Little Boy and A
	  Little Girl
	Little Jack and
	  Little Jill
	My Johann

GRIEG, E.
  Peer Gynt
	Anitra's Boogie
	Anitra Swings
	Feats of the Piper
	Fool's Gold
	The Hall of the
	  Swingin' King
	In the Hall of the
	  Mountain King Cha
	  Cha Cha
	King of the Mountain
	March of Trollgers

186

Composer & Source	Title
GRIEG, E. Peer Gynt (Cont.)	Mother's Lament Mountain Kingery Strange Music Work Song
GRIEG, E. Scherzo in E	Midsummer's Eve
GRIEG, E. Sonata for Violin 2	Now
GRIEG, E. To a Water Lily	Bon Vivant
GRIEG, E. To Spring	Hymn of Betrothal
GRIEG, E. Waltz 2	Now
GRIEG, E. Woodland Wanderings	At Christmastime
GROFE, F. Grand Canyon Suite	"Philip Morris"
GROFE, F. Mississippi Suite	Daybreak
GROSS, W. Tenderly	"The Rosemary Clooney Show"

HANDEL, G.
  Concerto for Organ 13
   in F
	The Cuckoo and the
	Nightingale

HANDEL, G. Concerto Grosso 7	Hornpipe Concerto
HANDEL, G. Royal Fireworks Music	Figure in the Carpet

Composer & Source	Title
HANDEL, G. Traditional	The Lord's Prayer
HANDEL, G. Water Music	Figure in the Carpet
HANDEL, G. Xerxes	Holy Art Thou Largo
HANSON, H. Symphony 4	Requiem Symphony
HARRISON, A. In the Gloaming	"Young Widder Brown"
HATHAWAY, C. My True Story	"My True Story"
HAVE NAGILA Traditional (Hebrew)	Harvey and Sheila
HAYDN, F. The Creation	Creation
HAYDN, J. Dance 16	The Bagpipes
HAYDN, J. Minuet for Orchestra	Ox Minuet
HAYDN, J. Sonata for Piano in D	Haydn Seeks
HAYDN, J. String Quartet in B Flat	The Hunt Quartet
HAYDN, J. String Quartet in B Flat (Op. 76, #4)	The Sunrise
HAYDN, J. String Quartet in B Flat (Op. 103)	Swan Song

Composer & Source	Title

HAYDN, J.
  String Quartet in C
    (Op. 33, #3)
	The Bird

HAYDN, J.
  String Quartet in D
    (Op. 50, #6)
	Frog Quartet

HAYDN, J.
  String Quartet in D
    (Op. 64, #5)
	The Lark Quartet

HAYDN, J.
  String Quartet in D
    (Op. 76, #2)
	Witches' Minuet

HAYDN, J.
  String Quartet in E Flat
    (Op. 33, #2)
	The Joke

HAYDN, J.
  String Quartet in F
    (Op. 50, #5)
	Dream Quartet

HAYDN, J.
  String Quartet in F
    (Op. 77, #2)
	Wait Till the Clouds
	  Roll By

HAYDN, J.
  String Quartet in F
    (Op. 55, #2)
	Razor Quartet

HAYDN, J.
  String Quartet in G
    (Op. 33, #5)
	How Do You Do?

HAYDN, J.
  String Quartet in G
    (Op. 74, #3)
	The Rider

HAYDN, J. Symphony 30	Allelujah

Composer & Source	Title
HAYDN, J. Symphony 39	The "Fist" Symphony
HAYDN, J. Symphony 43	Mercury Symphony
HAYDN, J. Symphony 44	Funeral Symphony
HAYDN, J. Symphony 45	Candle Symphony Farewell Symphony
HAYDN, J. Symphony 48	Maria Theresa
HAYDN, J. Symphony 55	The Schoolmaster
HAYDN, J. Symphony 59	Fire Symphony
HAYDN, J. Symphony 72	The Hunt Symphony
HAYDN, J. Symphony 82	The Bear Symphony
HAYDN, J. Symphony 83	The Hen Symphony
HAYDN, J. Symphony 85	La Reine
HAYDN, J. Symphony 92	Oxford Symphony
HAYDN, J. Symphony 94	Surprise Symphony
HAYDN, J. Symphony 101	The Clock Symphony
HAYDN, J. Symphony 103	Drum Roll Symphony

Composer & Source	Title
HAYDN, J. Symphony in C	Toy Symphony
HAYDN, J. Trio 5 in G	Gypsy Rondo Gypsy Trio
HEBREW FOLK TUNE Traditional	And the Angels Sing Tzena, Tzena, Tzena
HENRY VIII, KING Greensleeves	Sir Greenbaum's Madrigal What Child Is This?
HERBERT, V. Ah, Sweet Mystery of Life	"Bachelor's Children"
HERRMANN, B. Studio One Theme	"Studio One"
HEUBURGER, R. The Opera Ball	The Kiss in Your Eyes Midnight Bells Suddenly
HINDEMITH, P. Noblissima Visione	St. Francis
HINDEMITH, P. Symphonic Metamorphoses on a Theme by Weber	Metamorphoses
HINDEMITH, P. Theme and Four Variations	Four Temperments
HIRSCH, L. Love Nest	"Ethel and Albert"
HOFFMAN, A. Heartaches	Headaches

Composer & Source	Title
HOW CAN I LEAVE THEE Traditional	"Stella Dallas"

HUMPERDINCK, E.
  Hansel and Gretel
	Angel's Serenade
	"Ford Sunday Evening
	  Hour"
	Hop Hop Hop
	Jubilation Waltz
	Partner Come and
	  Dance With Me

IVANOVICI, J.
  Danube Waves
  (Donauwellen)
	Anniversary Song

I'VE BEEN WORKING ON THE RAILROAD Traditional	"The Railroad Hour"
JAHRNFELT, A. Berceuse	Lonely Night

JUANITA
  Traditional
	"The Romance of
	  Helen Trent"

KALMAR, B.
  Hooray for Captain
  Spaulding
	"You Bet Your Life"

KERN, J.
  The Way You Look
  Tonight
	"Mr. and Mrs. North"

KEYES, N. Suite	Empty Chair
KHATCHATURIAN, A. Gayne	Lullaby Russe

LA MARE, E.
  Organ Andantino in
  D Flat
	Moonlight and Roses

Composer & Source	Title
LECUONA, E. Andalucia	The Breeze and I
LECUONA, E. Canto Karaboli	Jungle Drums
LECUONA, E. Damisela Encantadora	It's No Secret That I Love You
LECUONA, E. Malaguena	At the Crossing
LECUONA, E. Maria La O	Maria My Own
LECUONA, E. Para Vigo Me Voy	Say Si Si
LECUONA, E. Yo Nada Puedo Hacer	My Hopeful Heart
LEHAR, F. Count of Luxembourg	Carnival for Life Love Goodbye
LEHAR, F. Frasquita	My Little Nest of Heavenly Blue
LEHAR, F. Gypsy Love	Lessons in Love Love and Wine Love is Like the Rose Matrimony
LEHAR, F. Lalalaika	Magic of Your Love
LEHAR, F. The Merry Widow	At Maxim's Les Grisettes de Paris I Am Free The Legend of Vilia

Composer & Source	Title
LEHAR, F.	
The Merry Widow (Cont.)	Love in My Heart
	Magic Waltz
	Maxim's
	No One Thanks the Go-Between
	The Picture of Fidelity
	Something So Delightful
	You'll Love Love In Paree
LENARD, M.	
Saber Theme	"Saber of London"
LEONCAVALLO, R.	
Mattinata	No Love But Your Love
	Wake With The Dawn
	You're Breaking My Heart
LEONCAVALLO, R.	
Pagliacci	Laugh Cool Clown
	My Cousin Carus
	Paper Pagliacci
LIADOFF, A.	
Paraphrases for Four Hands	Chopsticks
LISZT, F.	
Concerto for Piano 1 in E Flat	Triangle Concerto
LISZT, F.	
Consolation	My Consolation
LISZT, F.	
Dance Hongroise	Gypsy Rhapsody

Composer & Source	Title
LISZT, F. Hungarian Dance 15 in A	Rakoczy March
LISZT, F. Hungarian Rhapsodies	Like Hungarian
LISZT, F. Liebestraum	Dream of Love Dreams of Love and You My Dream of Love Nightfall
LISZT, F. Mephisto Waltz	Devil Dance
LISZT, F. Piano Suite (second movement)	The Christmas Tree
LISZT, F. Les Preludes	Love Is A Lovely Illusion
LISZT, F. Rhapsody 2	Ebony Rhapsody
LITTLE BALL OF YARN Traditional	Anymore
LLEWELLYN, R. Highway Patrol Theme	"Highway Patrol"
LLEWELLYN, R. Martin Kane Theme	"Martin Kane"
LLEWELLYN, R. Sea Hunt Theme	"Sea Hunt"
LOCATELLI, P. Concerto Grosso (Op. 7, #6)	Ariadne's Lament
LOMBARDO, C. Seems Like Old Times	"Arthur Godfrey Time"

Composer & Source	Title
LONDONDERRY AIR Traditional	Danny Boy "The Danny Thomas Show" "The O'Neill's"
LUBIN, H. Dear Loretta	"The Loretta Young Show"
LUCAS, C. The Perfect Song	"Amos 'n' Andy"
MAC DOWELL, E. Suite 2 in E (Op. 48)	Indian Suite
MC INTYRE, M. Suite	Whose Dream Are You
MAHLER, G. Kindertotenlieder	Dark Elegies
MAHLER, G. Symphony 1	Titan Symphony
MAHLER, G. Symphony 2	Resurrection Symphony
MAHLER, G. Symphony 7	Song of the Night
MARCHETTI, F. Waltz Tzigane	Fascination Automation

MARIE, G.
La Cinquantaine
	The Girl With the
	   Light Blue Hair
	"I Remember Mama"
	   Theme

MARTIN, H. Breezy and Easy	"The Patrice Munsel Show"

Composer & Source	Title
MARTINI, J. Plasir d'Amour	My Love Loves Me
MASCAGNI, P. Cavalleria Rusticanna	Almighty Lord Anthem For Spring Encore Melody
MASSENET, J. Elegie	To My Beloved
MASSENET, J. Meditation	Whisper a Word of Love
MATILDA Traditional	My Zelda
MENDELSSOHN, F. Fantasie in F Sharp	Scotch Sonata
MENDELSSOHN, F. Hear My Prayer	O For the Wings of A Dove
MENDELSSOHN, F. Midsummer Night's Dream	Starry Night of Splendor
MENDELSSOHN, F. On Wings of Song	On Song's Bright Pinions
MENDELSSOHN, F. Song Without Words	Little Suite
MENDELSSOHN, F. Piano Piece in A (Op. 19, #3)	Hunting Song
MENDELSSOHN, F. Piano Piece in A (Op. 19, #4)	Confidence

Composer & Source	Title
MENDELSSOHN, F. Piano Piece in A (Op. 62, #6)	Mendelssohn's Spring Song
MENDELSSOHN, F. Piano Piece in A (Op. 85, #8)	The Return
MENDELSSOHN, F. Piano Piece in A (Op. 102, #5)	Joyous Peasant
MENDELSSOHN, F. Piano Piece in A Flat (Op. 53, #1)	On the Shore
MENDELSSOHN, F. Piano Piece in A (Op. 19, #2)	unlisted
MENDELSSOHN, F. Piano Piece in B Flat (Op. 67, #3)	The Pilgrims
MENDELSSOHN, F. Piano Piece in B Flat (Op. 85, #6)	Song of the Traveler
MENDELSSOHN, F. Piano Piece in B (Op. 30, #4)	The Wanderer
MENDELSSOHN, F. Piano Piece in B (Op. 67, #5)	Shepherd's Complaint

Composer & Source	Title
MENDELSSOHN, F. Piano Piece in B Flat (Op. 30, #2)	Without Repose
MENDELSSOHN, F. Piano Piece in C (Op. 67, #4)	Spinning Song
MENDELSSOHN, F. Piano Piece in C (Op. 102, #3)	Tarantelle
MENDELSSOHN, F. Piano Piece in C (Op. 102, #6)	Faith
MENDELSSOHN, F. Piano Piece in C (Op. 38, #2)	Lost Happiness
MENDELSSOHN, F. Piano Piece in D (Op. 102, #3)	Retrospection
MENDELSSOHN, F. Piano Piece in E (Op. 19, #1)	Sweet Remembrance
MENDELSSOHN, F. Piano Piece in E (Op. 30, #3)	Consolation
MENDELSSOHN, F. Piano Piece in E (Op. 38, #3)	The Harp of the Post
MENDELSSOHN, F. Piano Piece in E (Op. 62, #3)	Funeral March
MENDELSSOHN, F. Piano Piece in E Flat (Op. 30, #1)	Contemplation

Composer & Source	Title

MENDELSSOHN, F.
  Piano Piece in E Flat
    (Op. 38, #1)
	Evening Star

MENDELSSOHN, F.
  Piano Piece in E Flat
    (Op. 85, #3)
	Passion

MENDELSSOHN, F.
  Piano Piece in F
    (Op. 53, #4)
	The Sorrowful Soul

MENDELSSOHN, F.
  Piano Piece in F
    (Op. 85, #1)
	Reverie

MENDELSSOHN, F.
  Piano Piece in F Sharp
    (Op. 19, #5)
	Restlessness

MENDELSSOHN, F.
  Piano Piece in F Sharp
  (Op. 67, #1)
	Lost Illusion

MENDELSSOHN, F.
  Piano Piece in F
    (Op. 62, #1)
	May Breezes

MENDELSSOHN, F.
  Piano Piece in F
    (Op. 62, #4)
	Morning Song

MENDELSSOHN, F.
  Piano Piece in G
    (Op. 53, #3)
	Agitation

MENDELSSOHN, F.
  Piano Piece in G
    (Op. 102, #4)
	Sighing Wind

MENDELSSOHN, F. Scherzo in E	Little Trumpet Piece

Composer & Source	Title

MENDELSSOHN, F.
  Song Without Words
    (Op. 67)
	The Bee's Wedding

MENDELSSOHN, F. Symphony 2	Hymn of Praise
MENDELSSOHN, F. Symphony 3	Scotch Symphony
MENDELSSOHN, F. Symphony 4	Italian Symphony
MENDELSSOHN, F. Symphony 5	Reformation Symphony

MENDELSSOHN, F.
  Traditional
	Let Saints on Earth
	  in Concert Sing

MENDELSSOHN, F. Witches' Song	Another May Song
MERRILY WE ROLL ALONG Traditional	"Truth or Consequences"
MEXICAN HAT DANCE Traditional (Mexico)	Oh Boy
MEYERBEER, G. Le Prophete	"A Tale of Today"
MOLLOY, J. Kerry Dancers	"Pretty Kitty Kelly"
MONTE, V. Czardas	Tambarina
MOVEL, G. Norwegian Cradle Song	Drowsy Baby

MOZART, W. A.
  Concerto for Violin 5
    in A
	Turkish Concerto

Composer & Source	Title
MOZART, W. A. Contradanse for Orchestra (K. 534)	The Thunderstorm
MOZART, W. A. Divertimento 15	Caracole
MOZART, W. A. Divertimento 17	Minuet in 4
MOZART, W. A. Don Giovanni	Hold My Hand, Giovanni Rockin' Don
MOZART, W. A. Eine Kleine Nachtmusik	A Little Night Jazz
MOZART, W. A. Magic Flute	I Catch the Birds from Dawn to Dark Samba Papageno
MOZART, W. A. Marriage of Figaro	Figaro Flip Nail In the Horseshoe
MOZART, W. A. Rondo alla Turca	Moe Zart's Turkey Trot Mozart's Turkish Trott Swing a la Turca Turkish Moon
MOZART, W. A. Serenade 9 in D	Post Horn Serenade
MOZART, W. A. Sonata for Piano 3 in C	The Harpsichord Player In An Eighteenth Century Drawing Roo: Somewhere

Composer & Source	Title

MOZART, W. A.
  Sonata for Piano 11
    in A
	Lullaby for Wolfgang

MOZART, W. A.
  Sonata for Piano 15
    in C
	In An Eighteenth
	    Century Drawing Room

MOZART, W. A. Symphony 31	Paris Symphony
MOZART, W. A. Symphony 35	Haffner Symphony
MOZART, W. A. Symphony 36	Linz Symphony
MOZART, W. A. Symphony 38	Prague Symphony
MOZART, W. A. Symphony 40	G Minor Cha Cha Mozart Goes Forty
MOZART, W. A. Symphony 41	Jupiter Symphony
M'SIEU BANJO Traditional (Creole)	Mister Taptoe

MUSSORGSKY, M.
  A Night on Bald
    Mountain
	"Escape"

MUSSORGSKY, M.
  Pictures At An
    Exhibition
	Hut of Baba Yaga

NEOPOLITAN NIGHTS unlisted	"The First Nighter"

NICOLAI, O.
  The Merry Wives of
    Windsor
	Marcheta

Composer & Source	Title
NIELSEN, C. Symphony 2	Four Temperments
NOBLE, R. Indian Suite	How Bright the Stars

OFFENBACH, J.
  La Belle Helene
	The Glory That Was
	    Greece
	Lament
	A Love-Sick Serenade
	O God of Love
	Vive la Virtue
	Whatever That May Be
	Love at Last

OFFENBACH, J. Bluebeard	Eureka

OFFENBACH, J.
  Gaite Parisienne
	Can-Can Boogie
	Can-Can Polka
	Shall We Say Farewell
	    to Spring

OFFENBACH, J. General de Brabant	The Greek Marines

OFFENBACH, J.
  Lischen et Freischen
	Never Bedevil the
	    Devil

OFFENBACH, J.
  Orpheus in the
    Underworld
	Brunswick Maine
	Busy Bee
	Comes the Revolution
	Five Minutes of
	    Spring
	How Soon, Oh Moon?
	Never Trust a Virgin
	An Old Love Dies

Composer & Source	Title
OFFENBACH, J. La Perichole	The Happiest Girl in the World
OFFENBACH, J. Tales of Hoffman (Barcarolle)	Adrift on a Star Barca Rock 'N Roll Barcarolle Blarney Barky Roll Stomp Beautiful Night Everytime I Try to Say Goodbye Hot Barcarolle Hurrah for Paree Never Let Me Go O Lovely Night Thwarted Thwarted, Curses, Curses Why Should We Deny Our Love
OFFENBACH, J. Themes	Gaite Parisienne
OFFENBACH, J. La Vie Parisienne	The Oath Politics
OH TANNENBAUM Traditional	Maryland, My Maryland
OI NEH CHODEH HRETCHEW Traditional	Yes My Darling Daughter
OLCOTT, C. My Wild Irish Rose	"Abie's Irish Rose"
ORTOLANI, R. Mondo Cane	More

Composer & Source	Title
PADEREWSKI, I. Minuet in G	Minuet in Mambo Paddy's Minuet
PAGANINI, N. Caprice 9 in C	The Hunt
PAGANINI, N. Perpetual Motion	Canary Caprice Pagan Ninny Keep-'er Goin' Stomp Paganini At a Party Paganini in Rhythm Paganini Playtime
PAGANINI, N. Variations	"The First Piano Quartet"
PHILE, P. The Washington March	Hail Columbia
POLIAKIN, R. Le Canari	The Hot Canary
POLLY WOLLY DOODLE Traditional	"Just Plain Bill"
PONCE, M. Estrellita	"Valiant Lady"

PONCHIELLI, A.
La Gioconda
	Ballet Cha Cha Cha
	Dancing Doll
	La Gioconda's Last
	  Dance
	Hello Muddah, Hello
	  Faddah

PROKOFIEV, S. Classical Symphony	Gala Performance

Composer & Source	Title
PROKOFIEV, S. Concerto for Piano 3	Gala Performance

PROKOFIEV, S.
  Love for Three Oranges
	"The FBI in Peace and
	  War"
	Three Oranges

PROKOFIEV, S.
  Peter and the Wolf
	Be Glad There's A Hole
	  In Your Head
	Dingbat, The Singing
	  Cat
	Magical Morn
	PeeWee and the Wolf
	Peter and the Wolf
	Rabbit Dance
	Tale of Peter and the
	  Wolf
	They Can't Catch Me
	Water Music

PROKOFIEV, S. Winter Holiday	Departure
PROZOROVSKY, B. Kak Stranno	How Strange
PUCCINI, G. La Boheme	Don't You Know My Love For You You
PUCCINI, G. Gianni Schicchi	Strolling Promenade
PUCCINI, G. Madama Butterfly	Cho Cho San Just A Dream Ago

Composer & Source	Title
PUCCINI, G.	
Tosca	Avalon
	Starlight Aria
PURCELL, H.	
The Gordian Knot Untied	Jig
	The Moor's Pavan
RACHMANINOFF, S.	
Concerto for Piano 1	Anya
RACHMANINOFF, S.	
Concerto for Piano 2	And Still the Volga Flows
	Before
	Full Moon and Empty Arms
	I Think of You
	I Will Bring You Music
	If This is Goodbye
	Rockin' With Rocky
	This Is My Kind of Love
RACHMANINOFF, S.	
Concerto for Piano 3	So Proud
RACHMANINOFF, S.	
Etudes Tableaux 2 (Op. 33)	Anya
RACHMANINOFF, S.	
Op. 4, #3	In the Silence of the Night
RACHMANINOFF, S.	
Polka Italienne	Vodka! Vodka!
RACHMANINOFF, S.	
Prelude in c Sharp	The Bells
	Russian Rag

Composer & Source	Title
RACHMANINOFF, S. Prelude in c Sharp (Cont.)	That Prelude The Bells of Moscow
RACHMANINOFF, S. Prelude in G (Op. 23)	Homeward Leben Sie Wohl
RACHMANINOFF, S. Rhapsody on a Theme of Paganini	Rachmaninoff Meets Paganini Paganini Rhapsody
RACHMANINOFF, S. Quartet for Strings in G	On That Day
RACHMANINOFF, S. Romance 3	Through the Silent Night
RACHMANINOFF, S. Songs(6)	At Night Here Beauty Dwells
RACHMANINOFF, S. Suite for Two Pianos	Hand in Hand Now Is My Moment
RACHMANINOFF, S. Symphony 1	All Hail the Empress So Proud
RACHMANINOFF, S. Symphony 2	Quiet Land
RACHMANINOFF, S. Vocalise 14 (Op. 34)	Little Hands Misty Days, Lovely Nights
RAINGER, R. Love In Bloom	"The Jack Benny Program"

Composer & Source	Title
RAINGER, R. Thanks for the Memory	"The Bob Hope Show"
RAPEE, E. Diane	"We Are Four"

RAVEL, M.
  L'Enfant et les
    Sortelieges
	Cat Duet

RAVEL, M.
  Pavan For A Dead
    Princess
	The Lamp Is Low
	Poco Pavane

RAVEL, M. La Valse	La Valse

RAVEL, M.
  Valses Nobles et
    Sentimentales
	Adelaide on la
	    Langage des Fleurs
	La Valse

RED RIVER VALLEY Traditional	"Our Gal Sunday"

RESPIGHI, O.
  Ancient Airs & Dances
	Three Virgins and a
	    Devil

RIMSKY-KORSAKOV, N. Capriccio Espagnole	Gypsy Dance Xanadu
RIMSKY-KORSAKOV, N. Christmas Eve Suite	Silver Bells
RIMSKY-KORSAKOV, N. Le Coq d'Or	Hymn To The Sun My Hymn To The Sun To Love A Dream

Composer & Source	Title
RIMSKY-KORSAKOV, N. Flight Of The Bumble Bee	The Bumble Beat Bumbling Bumblebee "The Green Hornet" The Rockin's Bee Sneezin' Bee
RIMSKY-KORSAKOV, N. The Hindu Song	Trees

RIMSKY-KORSAKOV, N.
  Paraphrases For Four
    Hands
	Chopsticks

RIMSKY-KORSAKOV, N.
  Scheherazade
	Arabian Nightmare
	Arabian Nights
	Charley's Dream
	Danse Orientale
	For The Love Of A
	    Princess
	Garden Of Love
	In The Hush Of The
	    Night
	Is It You
	Oriental Cha Cha Cha
	Prince And Princess
	Princess Scheherazade
	The Rest Of My Days
	Scheherazade Blue
	Sherabop
	A Thousand And One
	    Nights
	A Time, A Place, A Girl
	To Hora's Aid
	"Arabesque"

Composer & Source	Title
RIMSKY-KORSAKOV, N. Song of India	The Bossa India Play That "Song of India" Again
RIMSKY-KORSAKOV, N. Symphony 2	Antar
RINGWALD, R. A Cigarette, Sweet Music And You	"Chesterfield Supper Club"
ROBINSON, A. Water Boy	Seltzer Boy
ROCK-A-BYE BABY Traditional	"The Baby Snooks Show"
RODGERS, R. Blue Moon	"Hollywood Hotel"
RODGERS, R. Victory At Sea	No Other Love
ROIG, G. Quierme Mucho	Yours
ROSAS, J. Over The Waves	The Loveliest Night Of The Year
ROSE, D. Holiday For Strings	Holiday For States "The Red Skelton Show"
ROSSINI, G. Barber Of Seville	Suspended Automation
ROSSINI, G. La Gazza Ladra (Overture)	Con Amore

Composer & Source	Title
ROSSINI, G. La Promessa	Lisa's Waltz
ROSSINI, G. La Scala di Seta	Con Amore

ROSSINI, G.
  El Signor Bruschino
    (Overture)
	Con Amore

ROSSINI, G. Stabat Mater	Near the Cross

ROSSINI, G.
  William Tell (Overture)
	Gallopade
	"The Lone Ranger"
	William Tell Rag
	William Tell Rides
	    Again

RUBINSTEIN, A.
  Melody In F
	Now There, Mr.
	    Rubinstein
	Pickin' Melody in F
	Welcome Sweet
	    Springtime

RUBINSTEIN, A. The Old Refrain	Rubinstein's Refrain

RUBINSTEIN, A.
  Romance In E Flat
	If You Are But A
	    Dream

RUSSIAN FOLK SONG Traditional	Ivy Rose
SAINT-SAENS, C. Carnival Of The Animals	The Elephant

SAINT-SAENS, C.
  Concerto For Piano 5
    In F
	The Egyptian Concerto

Composer & Source	Title
SAINT-SAENS, C. Danse Macabre	Dance Of The Skeletons Dancing Skeletons
SAINT-SAENS, C. Omphale's Spinning Wheel	"The Shadow"
SAINT-SAENS, C. Samson And Delilah	When I Write My Song
SAINT-SAENS, C. The Swan (La Cygne)	Blue Is My Heart Swan's Song
SAINT-SAENS, C. Symphony 3	Organ Symphony
SAINT-SAENS, C. Valse Caprice (Op. 76)	Wedding Cake
SALAMA, A. Two Guitars	"The A & P Gypsies"
SANDERS, I. Adios Muchachos	I Get Ideas
SCARLATTI, D. Serenata	Though Light Is My Heart
SCARLATTI, D. Sonata For Piano In G	Cat's Fugue
SCARLATTI, D. Sonata For Piano (L. 23)	Cortege
SCARLATTI, D. Sonata for Piano (L. 132)	Barcarolle

Composer & Source	Title

SCARLATTI, D.
  Sonata For Piano
    (L. 488)
	The Bullfinch

SCHOENBERG, A. Verklaerte Nacht	Pillar Of Fire

SCHUBERT, F.
  Divertissment a la
    Hongroise
	March

SCHUBERT, F. Der Erlkonig	The Erl-King
SCHUBERT, F. Fantasy 15 In D (Op. 15)	Wanderer Fantasy
SCHUBERT, F. Liebestraum	Dream Of Love

SCHUBERT, F.
  Lilac Time
	Dream Enthralling
	The Flower
	The Golden Song
	Under The Lilac
	  Bough
	When The Lilac Bloom
	  Incloses

SCHUBERT, F. Nachtigall	Hark, Hark The Lark

SCHUBERT, F.
  Quartet For Strings 14
    (Op. 161)
	Death And The Maiden

SCHUBERT, F. Quintet In A (Op. 114)	Trout Quintet
SCHUBERT, F. Serenade	The Little Magician Our Serenade Serenade

Composer & Source	Title
SCHUBERT, F. Serenade (Cont.)	Stars Never Cry Top Of The Moon Twangy Serenade
SCHUBERT, F. Symphony 8	Hurried Tension Lalita Song Of Love

SCHUMANN, R.
  Concerto For Piano
    in A
	A Love Story

SCHUMANN, R. Du Bist Wie Eine Blume	How Like Unto A Flower
SCHUMANN, R. The Happy Farmer	There Once Was An Indian Maid
SCHUMANN, R. Ich Grolle Nicht	I'll Not Complain
SCHUMANN, R. Piano Piece(Op. 25, #7)	In God's Great Love
SCHUMANN, R. Sonata In D	Hurry
SCHUMANN, R. Symphony 1	Spring Symphony
SCHUMANN, R. Symphony 3	Rhenish Symphony
SCHUMANN, R. Traumerei	Dreaming Dreams Fantasy "Tony Wons Scrapbook"

Composer & Source	Title
SCHUMANN, R. Widmung	Dedication
SCHUMANN, R. Wild Horsemen	Wild Horses
SCHWARZ, A. This Is It	"The Aldrich Family"
SCHWARZ, A. You And I Know	"Front Page Farrell"
SEMPRINI, A. Mediterranean Concerto	Key To The Kingdom
SERESS, R. Szomoru Vasarnap	Gloomy Sunday
SHOSTAKOVICH, D. Symphony 2	October Symphony
SHOSTAKOVICH, D. Symphony 7	Leningrad Symphony
SIBELIUS, J. Finlandia	Accept Our Thanks Be Still My Soul Beloved Land Dear Land Of Home Eternal God, Our Father For Thee Suomi His World Shall Stand Morning Prayer O Morn Of Beauty O Singing Land On Great Lone Hills Through The Years We Would Be Building
SIBELIUS, J. Traditional	The Lord's Prayer Vale Of Shadow

Composer & Source	Title
SIBELIUS, J. Valse Triste	"I Love A Mystery"
SIMON, R. El Manisero	The Peanut Vendor
SLEEP unlisted	"The Fred Waring Show"
SMETANA, B. Quartet For Strings 1 In E	From My Life
SONG OF THE VOLGA BOATMAN traditional	The Vodka Boat Song
SOUSA, J. Stars And Stripes Forever	"National Farm And Home Hour"
SOVIET ARMY SONG Traditional (Russian)	Cavalry Of The Steppes
STEFFE, W. Battle Hymn Of The Republic	Ballad Of Harry Lewis
STEINER, M. Gone With The Wind	My Own True Love
STEINER, F. Perry Mason Theme	"Perry Mason"
STIGMAN, C. Dream Along With Me	"The Perry Como Show"
STRAUS, O. The Chocolate Soldier	After Today Just A Connoisseur

Composer & Source	Title
STRAUS, O. La Ronde	Love Makes The World Go Round
STRAUS, O. Waltz Dream	Love's Roundabout
STRAUSS, J. Alt Wien	Old Vienna Wien Swings
STRAUSS, J. Blue Danube Waltz	Black And Blue Danube Blue Danube Cha Cha Blue Danube Dream Blue Danube Goes Dixieland Blue Danube Lament Blue Danube Swing Greeting To Spring My Blue Danube Swingin' The Blue Danube
STRAUSS, J. Can-Can	Folies Bergere
STRAUSS, J. Emperor Waltz	Emperor Waltz
STRAUSS, J. Fledermaus	Chacun A Son Gout Girl With The Yellow Hair Laughing Song Look Me Over Once Love And Wine O My Dear Marquis Oh, What A Night Rosalinda

Composer & Source	Title
STRAUSS, J. The Great Waltz	Love Will Find You

STRAUSS, J.
  The Gypsy Baron
	Escape It All
	A Girl Is A
	  Necessary Trouble
	I Live To Love You

STRAUSS, J.
  A Night In Venice
	According To The
	  Baedeker
	I Can't Find My Wife

STRAUSS, J.
  Tales From The Vienna
  Woods
	Vienna Woods Cha Cha
	Cha

STRAUSS, J. Three Waltzes	I Found My Love

STRAUSS, R.
  Burleske For Piano
  And Orchestra
	Dim Lustre

STRAVINSKY, I. Concerto Grosso In D	The Cage

STRAVINSKY, I.
  Firebird Suite
	Lullaby Of The
	  Firebird
	Summer Moon

THE STREETS OF LAREDO Traditional	Streets Of Miami

STYNE, J.
  As Long As There's
  Music
	"The Eddie Fisher
	  Show"

STYNE, J.
  The Party's Over
	"The Polly Bergen
	  Show"

Composer & Source	Title
STULTZ, R.	
The Sweetest Story Ever Told	"John's Other Wife"
SULLIVAN, A.	
HMS Pinafore	Admiral's Boogie
	Ah Well A Day
	All That Glitters
	Little Butterball
SULLIVAN, A.	
Ivanhoe	Ho Jolly Jenkins
SULLIVAN, A.	
The Mikado	The Jazz Mikado
	Tit Willow Twist
	You Need An Analyst
SULLIVAN, A.	
Pirates Of Penzance	Hail, Hail The Gang's All Here
SULLIVAN, A.	
Ruddigore	Sherlock Holmes
TALLIS, T.	
Tallis' Canon	Evening Hymn
TARTINI, G.	
Sonata For Violin In G	The Devil's Trill
TCHAIKOVSKY, P.	
Andante Cantabile	Recollections of Tchaikovsky
	"Road Of Life"
TCHAIKOVSKY, P.	
Capriccio Italien	No Place Like Rome
	So Help Me
TCHAIKOVSKY, P.	
Concerto For Piano 1	Concerto For Two
	Evening Concerto
	Lilacs And Love

221

Composer & Source	Title

TCHAIKOVSKY, P.
  Concerto For Piano 1
    (Cont.)
	No Greater Love
	Recollections Of
	  Tchaikovsky
	Some Song Tchaikovsky
	  Wrote
	Tonight We Love_
	Tonight You're Mine

TCHAIKOVSKY, P. Concerto For Piano 2	Ballet Imperial
TCHAIKOVSKY, P. Concerto For Piano 3	Allegro Brilliante
TCHAIKOVSKY, P. Marche Slave	Song Of The Steppes
TCHAIKOVSKY, P. The Months	April Snowbell August Harvest Song Balalaika Serenade June Barcarolle

TCHAIKOVSKY, P.
  None But The Lonely
    Heart
	For Every Lonely
	  Heart
	How Long Wilt Thou
	  Forget Me
	"Kitty Keene"

TCHAIKOVSKY, P.
  Nutcracker Suite
	Arabesque Cookie
	Blue Reeds
	China Where
	Chinoiserie
	Dance For Young Lovers
	Dance Of The Floreadores
	Dance Of The Orange
	  Tarts

Composer & Source	Title

TCHAIKOVSKY, P.
  Nutcracker Suite (Cont.)
	Danse Mistique
	Flower Waltz
	I Guess I'll Have To
	  Go On Dreaming
	Like Nutty Overture
	The Magic Nutcracker
	March Of The Sugar
	  Plummers
	Nutcracker Suite Goes
	  Latin
	Nutty Marche
	Orchestra In A
	  Nutcracker Shell
	Overture For Shorty
	Peanut Brittle Brigade
	Sugar Plum Cha Cha
	Sugar Rum Cherry
	The Swinging Plum
	  Fairy
	Toot Toot Tootie Toot
	Volga Vouty

TCHAIKOVSKY, P. Quartet In D	The Isle Of May Stolen Kisses

TCHAIKOVSKY, P.
  Romance
	These Are The Things
	  I Love

TCHAIKOVSKY, P. Romeo And Juliet	Dear One Forever Loved Juliet's Farewell Our Love Romeo And Juliet "Passing Parade"

Composer & Source	Title
TCHAIKOVSKY, P. Russian Church Service	I Believe In One God The Lord's Prayer O Come Let Us Worship
TCHAIKOVSKY, P. Serenade For Strings	Waltz Serenade
TCHAIKOVSKY, P. Sextet In D (Op. 70)	Souvenir Of Florence
TCHAIKOVSKY, P. Sleeping Beauty	Aurora's Wedding I Wonder Love's Own Waltz Once Upon A Dream
TCHAIKOVSKY, P. Song	Immortal Song
TCHAIKOVSKY, P. Song Without Words	Kiss Me Tonight Night Wind
TCHAIKOVSKY, P. Suite 3	Theme And Variations
TCHAIKOVSKY, P. Swan Lake	Daydreaming Of A Night More Than Anything Stolen Kisses Swan Song Swan Splashdown Swan Swings Warm Kisses In The Cool of the Night
TCHAIKOVSKY, P. Symphony 1	Winter Dreams

Composer & Source	Title
TCHAIKOVSKY, P. Symphony 2	Little Russian Symphony
TCHAIKOVSKY, P. Symphony 3	Polish Symphony
TCHAIKOVSKY, P. Symphony 5	Backbeat Symphony Long May We Love Lovers By Starlight Moon Love Pete's Fifth Save Me A Dream

TCHAIKOVSKY, P.
Symphony 6
	Always You
	Challenge
	No Star Is Lost
	Now And Forever
	Recollections Of
	  Tchaikovsky
	Story Of A Starry
	  Night
	Strings At The Hop
	Take Me Tonight
	You Are Remembered
	Pathetique Symphony
	"Road Of Life"

TCHAIKOVSKY, P. Trio In A (Second movement)	Designs With String
TE QUIERO DIJISTE Traditional (Spain)	Magic Is The Moonlight
THOMAS, A. Andante	Once In A Lifetime

225

Composer & Source	Title

TILZER, H. VON
  Just A Little Love,
    A Little Kiss
	"Life Of Mary
	  Sothern"

TOBANI, T. Hearts And Flowers	Once In May

TOSELLI, E.
  Serenade
	"The Goldbergs"
	Morning Noon and
	  Night
	Serenade
	Years and Years
	  Ago

TROTTER, J. S.
  Gobelues
	"The George Gobel
	  Show"

TRUMAN, E. Matinee Theater Theme	"Matinee Theater"
UKRANIAN FOLK SONG Traditional	Minka
UTRERA, A. Green Eyes	Green Stamps
VAUGHAN WILLIAMS, R. Symphony 1	Sea Symphony
VAUGHAN WILLIAMS, R. Symphony 2	London Symphony
VAUGHAN WILLIAMS, R. Symphony 7	Sinfonia Antarctica
VERDI, G. Aida	King Cotton O Native Land Pink Chiffon

Composer & Source	Title
VERDI, G. Rigoletto	Cute And Sassy Here Juanita Banana Musical Chairs Over The Summer Sea Rigoletto Rag Rigoletto Rock
VERDI, G. themes	The Lady And The Fool
VERDI, G. La Traviata	Provenza By The Sea
VERDI, G. Il Trovatore	Anvil Parade Blacksmith Rag Home To Our Mountain Sotto Voce
VIENI SUL MAR Traditional	Tara Talarra Talar

VILLA-LOBOS, H.
  The Theft Of The
    Madonna (Magdalena)
	Forbidden Orchid

VILLOLDO, A. El Choclo	Kiss Of Fire

VIVALDI, A.
  Concerto For String
    Orchestra In A
	Echo

VIVALDI, A. Concerto For Violin	Cuckoo Concerto
VOORHEES, D. The Bell Waltz	"The Telephone Hour"

Composer & Source	Title

WAGNER, R.
  Lohengrin
	Wedding Bouquet
	Where Did You Get
	  That Hat

WAGNER, R. Tannhauser	Hymn to Venus Star Of Evening
WALDTEUFEL, E. Dolores Waltz	All My Life
WEBER, C. Der Freischutz	Hunting Chorus
WEBER, C. Invitation To The Dance	Come To The Dance Spectre Of The Rose
WEBERN, A. Ricercata	Episodes

WEILL, K.
  The Threepenny Opera
	The Judgement Of
	  Paris

WEINBERGER, J.
  Midnight Bells
	Our Secret
	  Rendezvous

WHEN IT'S ROUNDUP TIME IN TEXAS unlisted	"Tom Mix"

WHITING, R.
  One Hour With You
	"The Eddie Cantor
	  Show"

WIENIAWSKI, H.
  Concerto For Violin
    In D
	Love Star

Composer & Source	Title
WILSON, M. 　You And I	"Maxwell House Coffee 　Time"
WILSON, S. 　Wells Fargo Theme	"Wells Fargo"
YRADIER, S. 　La Paloma	Be Mine
YRFEY 　A Knave Is A Knave	A Guy Is A Guy